Dance With the Spirits

By Debra Hughey

Wake Forest, NC

www.scuppernongpress.com

Dance With the Spirits
Debra Hughey

©2020 Debra Hughey

First Printing

The Scuppernong Press
PO Box 1724
Wake Forest, NC 27588
www.scuppernongpress.com

Cover and book design by Frank B. Powell, III

All rights reserved. Printed in the United States of America.

No part of this book may be reproduced or transmitted in any form or by any means, electronic or mechanical, including photocopying, recording, or by any information and storage and retrieval system, without written permission from the editor and/or publisher.

International Standard Book Number ISBN 978-1-942806-26-4

Library of Congress Control Number: 2020907819

Table of Contents

Foreword..1

Chapter One, Minnie Raintree, December 2018.........3
Chapter Two, Time to Go, August 1836......................7
Chapter Three, Grandmothers Will Guide the Way....13
Chapter Four, No More Money.................................17
Chapter Five, I Now Understand...............................21
Chapter Six, Silver Cross and White Beads................23
Chapter Seven, White Man Mischief.........................25
Chapter Eight, I Am Thirsty......................................27
Chapter Nine, We Will Soon Leave Alabama.............31
Chapter Ten, Hard Times and Sadness......................33
Chapter Eleven, I Will Take Her Flowers...................35
Chapter Twelve, Sweet Song of the Blue Bird............39
Chapter Thirteen, We Are Here.................................43
Chapter Fourteen, The Cold is Biting My Toes..........47
Chapter Fifteen, We Have Been Tricked Again..........51
Chapter Sixteen, I Am Morning Star.........................55
Chapter Seventeen, Grandmother and the Creek Stranger....59
Chapter Eighteen, The Man Called Hawk..................63
Chapter Nineteen, To the Canadian...........................67
Chapter Twenty, The Drumbeat, December 2018......69
Chapter Twenty-One, The Spirit Will Be with Us......73
Chapter Twenty-Two, Corn From the Horses............77
Chapter Twenty-Three, Dream of the Grandmothers...81
Chapter Twenty-Four, Green Corn Again..................83
Chapter Twenty-Five, A Dream.................................87

Chapter Twenty-Six, The Wedding Celebration.......................89

Chapter Twenty-Seven, Hot Chocolate and Cookies,
December 2018 95

Chapter Twenty-Eight, We Will Make Plans, 1842..................97

Chapter Twenty-Nine, Time to Go Home 101

Chapter Thirty, Sweet Brown Drink 103

Chapter Thirty-One, We Will Cross Over 107

Chapter Thirty-Two, Our People Will Not Be There..............111

Chapter Thirty-Three, Back Home on the Tallapoosa...........115

Chapter Thirty-Four, Return of the Owl, December 2018 ...121

Chapter Thirty-Five, Cemetery on the Hill, 1858 125

Chapter Thirty-Six, Soldiers of Blue and Gray 131

Chapter Thirty-Seven, There's Gonna Be Some Fight'n 135

Chapter Thirty-Eight, Hard Times in the Southland,
December 2018 139

Chapter Thirty-Nine, Dance of Minnie Raintree,
December 2018 143

Epilogue 149

Acknowledgments...151

Foreword

Dance with the Spirits is the fourth and final of the sequel of books that include *The Owl and the Horseshoe*, *Spirit of the Red Stick Women* and *Just a Cotton Field*. Our story began as the main characters Soaring Eagle and Little Flower, in the time of their youth, experienced the turbulent events prior to the Battle of Horseshoe Bend, then the horrors of the battle, the sorrow afterwards and the desperate period that led to their removal.

Dance with the Spirits is the culmination of the story and tells of the hardship of the "Trail Where They Cried" and how the Creek people, depending on the strength of the grandmothers persevered. Based on accurate historical facts, *Dance with the Spirits* intermingles the past with the present. Come with me now to a different time and be prepared for the unexpected.

Chapter One
December 2018
Minnie Raintree

The old house was small, very small. Remains of an old cotton field and large oak trees encroached on both sides. A little stream gurgled over rocks not far from the railed back porch. Matthew Walker slowed his old reliable truck as the little house, which was not more than a slightly remodeled cabin, came into view, gray smoke curling for the stone chimney. "Here, we are," Matthew said to the young man at his side. The two young men, already friends, had become much closer since the day of the fishing trip of the past summer. A bond of spirit had formed between the two, a spirit that had begun over two-hundred years ago.

Jacob East had sat in silence as they had slowly wound their way over the wide path that served as a road to the old cabin. He had no idea where they were or where they were going. Matthew had only said that he had someone he wanted him to meet and that he needed to bring his jacket and some old shoes. "This has been a fantastic ride. I have never been in a more beautiful or isolated place, except down by the river," Jacob said, staring in wonder at the little house. "Does someone really live here?"

"Yes, in fact, a relative of mine," Matthew answered, smiling at this friend.

"A relative, are you kidding me?" Jacob inquired.

"Nope, this is the home of my great, great aunt. Her name is Minnie Raintree Walker. She is one-hundred two years old and she lives right here by herself," Matthew proudly answered. "My family seems to have a long-life span," he continued.

"Who, who takes care of her?" Jacob asked in awe.

"Some cousins of mine live up on the main highway and they come check on her and bring food several times a week. She is absolutely amazing and a memory that you will not believe," Matthew said, as he stopped the old truck and reached

Dance With the Spirits

behind the seat for a large bag. "Come on, Aunt Minnie Raintree will be waiting on us and I think you will be very interested in what she has to say."

"What's in the bag, Matthew and why haven't you mentioned your aunt before? Does she know anything about your family history?" Jacob excitedly asked as he forced the old truck door open.

"Man, you do have lots of questions," Matthew laughed. "Sandwiches for us and Aunt Minnie Raintree to answer your first question. The time is now right for you to meet her and she not only knows about the family's Indian history, she is one. Now come on and remember to wipe your feet before we go in."

The wooden door opened before Matthew could knock and Minnie Raintree stood smiling at the two young men. "Matthew, you and your friend come on in now before you get cold. I have hot chocolate and cookies ready. I know that y'all are hungry," the old lady laughed, "boys are always hungry."

Matthew smiled at Jacob as his friend looked across the little room in amazement, the mixture of modern and the past creating a stark contrast. Baskets made from river cane and old pottery bowls shared space with dozens of brightly bound books on the shelves of a totally modern entertainment center. A college football game was loudly playing on a large digital TV.

Minnie Raintree laughed again, "What did you expect, a little old granny woman sitting in a rocking chair in the dark? Soon as Alabama scores again, I'll turn the game off." Looking at Jacob, she extended her hand. "I am sorry. Where are my manners? I am Minnie Raintree Walker. And you must be Jacob?"

"Yes mam, I am Jacob East," the young man said as he shook the woman's small hand, surprised at the strength in her grip. Trying not to rudely stare, Jacob realized that this woman, who had lived more than a century, looked remarkably healthy. Her gray hair hung down her back in a long braid and her jet-black eyes sparkled with strength and humor. Minnie Raintree's loosely fitting jeans and solid gray shirt were immaculate. Jacob could not help but stare at the string of blue beads that hung from her neck.

"Yes, my boy, these beads are real and were worn by my great grandmother," Minnie Raintree said, smiling broadly at Jacob. "I think you may have heard of her. Morning Star was her name. Come on now to the table and let's have some hot chocolate and some cookies. They are just out of the oven."

The old woman smiled at Matthew as she poured steaming hot chocolate into three heavy mugs, neatly placed on native designed hand-woven mats, which were arranged on a beautiful antique round table. "It is good to see you again. I have a surprise to tell you."

"I'm so happy to see you too, Aunt Minnie Raintree," Matthew said. "Hey, I brought us sandwiches. Do you want to eat them now or save them for later?"

"We can save them. I think y'all will be here for a while," Minnie Raintree excitedly replied. "In fact, I would like for the two of you to spend the night. I have so much I would like to talk about."

Matthew looked at Jacob as he picked up a large chocolate chip cookie from a platter that looked as old as his aunt. "What do you think buddy, got any other plans for tonight?"

"Nope, and I would love to stay, but where would we sleep," Jacob inquired, looking around the small house.

"Aunt Minnie Raintree has sleeping bags and we can sleep in front of the fire and the night sounds are fantastic," Matthew excitedly answered. He loved spending the night with his aunt and it had been a while since he had.

Jacob looked at the old woman who smiled at the two young men. "May I, ugh," Jacob stammered, "may I call you Aunt Minnie?"

"No, but you may call me Aunt Minnie Raintree," she replied. "That is my name. Oh, we are going to have a fine time. I believe the reason y'all came to see me is to hear about the family of Matthew and me. Is that correct?"

"Yes mam, it is. I am fascinated about Matthew's family," Jacob answered as he grabbed a cookie.

"Well then, sit down and I will begin, but let me set the stage so you can completely understand," the old woman said, taking a sip of hot chocolate. "As you now know, my name is Minnie Raintree Walker. I was born in the year 1916 under a big tree, not far from here," she smiled. "It was raining very hard. My mother was born in 1878, and her mother was born in 1852. She was the last child of Morning Star," she paused again, taking another drink from her mug. "And if you are wondering how Matthew and me can have the same last name, well that's simple and I'll explain that a little bit further along in my story. The Walkers were from the same family line as old Trader Walker who married a relative of Chief Big Warrior from Tuckabatchee. I do need to slow down now and not get ahead of myself." Minnie Raintree paused, taking Matthew's hand, "My boy, I have been writing the family history down. It needs to be preserved. Since you have a great interest in our heritage, and even more, I believe you have the spirit of our people within you, I want you to have it when it is completed." Pausing again, the old lady shivered, pretending to be cold. "Matthew would you and Jacob mind going out on the back porch and bringing in some more wood for the fire. I do feel chilled. Then we can move back to the living room and I will continue. I do believe Jacob, that Matthew has already told you our story, beginning with the time of the Horseshoe and the owl, and how the spirit of our women helped my people to survive and then the sad time before they were forced to leave their home. I'll begin there when y'all come back in and tell of the hard times our people endured on the trail where they cried, and of making new homes in Indian Territory and how the people split again when the big war came. Then I will tell you how I ended up here in this little house back in Alabama. I'll begin my story with Soaring Eagle, the father of my great grandmother. Soaring Eagle. ...

Chapter Two
August 31, 1836
Time to Go

Soaring Eagle watched in sadness as the women slowly climbed on to the wagons, tears rolling down their brown faces, many of them keening in the ancient way of sorrow. His heart was heavy as he realized that this was the day, that he had known for many, many seasons, would come. He and his people had tried valiantly to save their land. They had fought bravely and lost too many of their warriors. They had tried to live among the white people who came in great numbers to the land that belonged to them. They had tried to live under the laws of these people to preserve the home of the grandfathers. They had even pleaded. The former chieftain of the Hillabee felt the lump in his throat and the sting of unshed tears in his eyes. They had lost the battle, not only on the battlefield but the battle to keep their land. They had lost their home, and this was the day they would leave. He turned one final time to gaze at the river. Oh, the Tallapoosa, the river of pulverized rocks, the cat in the cane break, the river of fawns. The river that had been the life source for the Creek people since before the time of the grandfathers, grandfathers. Even now just watching the rapid flow of the shinning river seemed to give Soaring Eagle the strength and courage that he so desperately needed.

Feeling the slight tap on his shoulder, Soaring Eagle turned to face his daughter. "My father," the beautiful young maiden said softly. "My brother, Fox Slayer sends word to you that Chief Opothle Yahola is ready for us to go and he needs for you to be among the leaders." Morning Star smiled at her father, understanding the tremendous pain he was feeling. Her eyes glistened as she reached into the beaded bag, touching the doll with no eyes that her father had given her so long ago. She could feel the green stone Uncle Badger gave her for courage along with the gifts from old Sinnugee, the crystal and the wooden owl. She pulled the crystal from the pouch and red immediately streaked the clear stone. "Father, look. My crystal is red," Morning Star said as tears slid down her face. "This means our journey to Indian Territory will be filled with sorrow." She pulled the green stone from the bag and held it tightly.

With a final look at the river, Soaring Eagle took the small hand of his youngest daughter. "Do not fear, my child," he consoled, "the Spirit of the grandmothers will guide our way and our people will survive." He paused to regain his composure before joining his people. "Yes, it is time for us to leave our home, the home of our grandfathers. I do feel in my heart that our people will one day return. Our spirit will never leave this place." As the two walked side by side to join their family, the familiar coo of the dove and the late season song of the redbird filled the air, only to be replaced by the melancholy call of the owl.

Soaring Eagle walked pass the long line of wagons, the iron pots and pans obtained from the white man dangling from the sides. Many of the Tuckabatchee had accumulated much over the past few seasons and the wagons were packed with personal belongings, barely leaving room for the women and children. His people had very little, having been ordered by gun point to take only what could be carried when they were forced from their Hillabee home. He noticed as he neared the front of the wagon line that his daughter, Morning Star was no longer by his side. Not being alarmed, he knew that she, as she always had, would need a time to commune with the grandmothers, the Spirit of those that would be left behind. She would catch up with the others when she was ready. Seeing that Chief Opothle Yahola was waiting for him near the front, Soaring Eagle paused only briefly at the wagon of his family to speak to Little Flower and untie his brown and white Indian pony. Taking her outreached hand, he softly whispered, "My Little Flower, today we will begin our journey to a new and different land. We will leave our beloved home, the home of the grandfathers." He gently wiped away the tears that slowly ran down her cheek, seeing the sorrow and strength that filled her huge brown eyes. "My beautiful flower, we will again be happy. The Spirit of the grandmothers will help us along the way. I must go now. I, as well as Fox Slayer, Horse Stealer and Badger have been chosen to lead our people. I will return when we camp for the night." Looking at his grandson who was quickly becoming a young warrior, he continued, "Coyote, take care of your mother and grandmother and keep your sister, Blue Bird out of mischief. Be strong and remember we are Creek and we will survive this difficult time."

Soaring Eagle noticed that several white men, one dressed as a white soldier, stood talking with Chief Opothle Yahola. Just as he joined the men, his son Fox Slayer, the husband of the chief's daughter, Horse Stealer and his close friend Badger, appeared by his side. "Ah, Soaring Eagle," Chief Opothle Yahola greeted Soaring Eagle. "I see that you and these trusted men are prepared," looking at Fox Slayer, he continued, "My son, is your wife and my grandson comfortably settled in for the journey?"

"Yes, my chief. They are with her mother in the wagon just ahead of my mother and sister. They are ready when the word is given for us to go," Fox Slayer answered, glancing at the white men.

"Good," Opothle Yahola said, "These men will assist us with our journey. Mr. Ingersoll on behalf of the Alabama Emigrating Party will oversee the details. Mr. Bateman with the Army of the South, United States Infantry, will make sure everything is done as the government has provided. Dr. Bussy from Tallassee will be available to care for any who fall sick and attend to injuries that occur along the way. And finally, my friend and advisor Mr. Barrent Dubois. I think you are already acquainted with him. Mr. Dubois is the assistant agent."

Soaring Eagle and the others extended their hand in white man fashion to the man who would guide them to their new home in Indian Territory. Each of them were slightly apprehensive, but in the manner of Creek, the white government men were totally unaware of their discomfort.

Speaking with authority and looking at Mr. Ingersoll, Soaring Eagle clearly and loudly said, "Sir, my people are ready to depart. We will follow your instructions."

"That is good. We will begin very shortly and" … before Ingersoll finished speaking several men on large black stallions rode up in a cloud of dust, stopping just short of the group of men.

"These injuns ain't going nowhere right now," a ruddy faced man with a badge on his tightly fitting shirt yelled out.

"What is the meaning of this?" Ingersoll questioned as one of the other riders pulled a pistol from his saddle bag.

"I am sheriff of this part of Tallapoosa County and I have warrants for the arrest of" … looking down at a torn, dirty piece of paper he had pulled from his pocket, he continued. "Shoot, I can't say these names, but I know who they are anyway."

"What have they done? What law have they broken," Opothle Yahola asked with anger fleeting across his handsome face.

"Well, they, they are horse thieves. They stole horses from some of the white farmers over Tallassee way. And some of 'em owe money down at the factory store," the sheriff stammered, obviously not telling the truth.

"Give me the paper," Ingersoll said shortly, taking the paper from the sheriff, he continued. "Chief Opothle Yahola, do you know these men?"

"Yes, the chief answered, "none of them would take the horse of any man and these that are accused of owing a debt have money to pay for what they want."

"Soaring Eagle take your men here and go find these people who are charged. Bring them back and we will get to the bottom of this. We do not need any more delays," Ingersoll ordered, plainly irritated with the situation.

The sun was directly overhead when Soaring Eagle returned with eight Tuckabatchee and four Tallassee headmen.

None of them were in a pleasant mood when they were told of the accusations.

"My Chief," Soaring Eagle addressed Opothle Yahola. "Here are the men you asked me to bring. Our people are hungry. I told them to eat only bread already prepared. We do not have time to unpack and cook."

"That was good," Opothle Yahola said smiling faintly. "I know our people are becoming restless."

"Yes, and there's more," Soaring Eagle said softly. "Some of the white men camped near us have sold our young warriors their fire water. I am afraid some of them are very drunk."

"Oh no, not the fire water!" Opothle Yahola exclaimed. "Do not let Ingersoll and the others know about this. Go quickly and dunk their heads in the river. We are not getting off to a good start. We do not need for this to happen. Our people will all return to their old homes if given the opportunity."

It was mid-afternoon before the sheriff would allow the accused men to go and only then after several gold coins had exchanged hands and the trumped-up charges dropped. The sheriff tipped his hat and smiled as he put the coins in his shirt pocket. Both the white government men and the Creek leaders glared at the unscrupulous sheriff, knowing that an unjust deed had occurred, one they knew would happen time after time along the way to Indian Territory.

Chapter Three
Grandmothers Guided the Way

The sheriff and his band of deputies had left, the drunken young warriors had been sobered and finally the word was given to begin. The forlorn Creek people, their dark faces set in stoic expressions, faced forward as the long line of wagons began slowly to move. No one looked back, no one spoke, no child whimpered, and the chirping songbirds had become quiet. No was surprise when the silence was broken by the melancholy call of the owl. The owl, with his cry of sadness, had appeared to them long before the big battle at the Horseshoe and had continued to visit them during times of trouble. The people now expected to hear the familiar sound and had learned that the winged creature was preparing them for what was to come. They were ready.

The sun was well past the mid-point in the crystal blue afternoon sky before all the wagons had begun the first phase of the journey. The people rode in watchful silence, most having a sick feeling in the pits of their stomach, a feeling of uncertainty and one just short of fear. Before the Creek people had traveled out of the area that was familiar to them, only six miles from the starting point of Pole Cat Springs, the word was called out to stop. Orders were given to make camp for the night, using only the barest of essentials as a early morning start was planned.

Soaring Eagle, Fox Slayer and Horse Stealer made their way back to the wagons of their families. Badger, having no family, would have his meals with Soaring Eagle, Little Flower and their daughter, Morning Star. Little Flower had started the fire and had stew boiling in the iron pot when Soaring Eagle returned to her wagon, her face lighting up with the love she felt for her husband. Badger watched, still experiencing a fleeting of the love he still had for the beautiful woman who after the time of the Horseshoe had stolen his heart. He knew that if Soaring Eagle had not survived the battle, she would be his wife. He scolded himself for his thoughts and noticed that she seemed upset.

"Soaring Eagle," Little Flower called out, her voice quivering in fear, "She is not here! Morning Star is not here!"

Frowning himself, Soaring Eagle gently took his wife in his arms and held her close. This had been a very trying day and he knew that the area was crawling with evil white men that would think nothing of harming his daughter. She had no idea of her beauty. "I talked with her before we left Pole Cat Springs. That was before we were stopped by the sheriff. She said she would catch up with us," Soaring Eagle said softly. "You know how she communes with the grandmothers. Come Badger, we will go in search of her and if any man has harmed her, may the God of the white man help him, because he will suffer."

Soaring Eagle and Badger, walking in silence, retraced their steps. When the last rays of the setting sun began to fade behind the western tree line, they saw her. Morning Star, holding the hand of a frightened little boy, his dirty face streaked with tears and dried blood on his arms, both quickly walking toward them. Seeing her father, Morning Star dropped the child's hand and ran to her father.

"My father, my father," she cried out with rare tears falling freely from her huge brown eyes. "I am happy to see you!"

"Morning Star, my daughter, have you been harmed?" The worried father questioned. "Where have you been?" Looking at the child with her, he continued, "And who is the little boy with you? He has been injured."

Smiling, as she wiped away her tears, Morning Star slowly began. "Father, I have not been harmed. The name of my new little friend is Turtle Boy. He fell as we were running through the woods looking for a place to hide."

"Why did you need to hide?" Badger quickly asked, with obvious anger in his voice.

"Uncle Badger, I am happy to see you also," Morning Star continued. "I, I stayed too long with the Grandmothers. I did not realize you had left. I found Turtle Boy standing near the wagon path," she continued, her voice quivering. "They saw us before we saw them, some of the evil white men who sell our people their fire water. Oh, my father they yelled such bad things, telling me what they would do to me." Morning Star paused as tears again ran down her cheek. She had seen sixteen summers and fully understood the intent of the white men. She had encountered similar situations before but none as serious at this. She had felt totally helpless, knowing there was no one to help her and nowhere to hide. Taking a deep breath and regaining her composure, the young maiden finished telling of the harrowing experience. She pointed to Turtle Boy, "I grabbed his hand and told him to run. I knew we could not stay on the wagon path and the men; I think there were four, were closing in on us. I prayed for the Giver of Breath to help me and for the grandmothers to guide the way. My father, suddenly a large red hawk flew over us and then I saw a tiny opening, the path of a deer, we darted inside. There was a little dip in the path and the men did not see us. This is where Turtle Boy fell and cut his arms. I placed my hand over his mouth so that he would not cry out," Smiling at the little boy, she continued. "He is very brave. He will make a good warrior one day. We waited in a little ravine as the men ran past us. They were yelling the bad words the white men like to say." Morning Star laughed, "and they all had big stomachs and had trouble breathing. Then my father, clouds covered the sun, where there had been no clouds and the wind blew cold and the call of the owl was loud. "She laughed again, "the white men stopped and looked at each other, then turned and began to run in the direction they had come. I think they are still running. Me and Turtle stayed in the woods for a while and then moved to the edge of the path. No one else tried to harm us. My father, I need to find his mother, I know she will worry."

"His mother is not the only mother that will worry," Soaring Eagle said as he hugged his daughter. "Come, let us return to the wagon. It is good that you were not harmed in any way."

"Yes," Badger, added. "The white men with the big stomachs would have suffered much on this day."

Chapter Four
No More Money

The pocket watch that hung from conductor Ingersoll's belt showed twenty minutes past eight, much later than he had hoped to have the wagons rolling. It had been difficult to get over one-thousand people up and moving. He realized this was only the beginning of their long journey and there would be many issues to deal with along the way. He hoped to get to Wetumpka today without any delays. The Creek, at least, seemed to be agreeable this morning and had not created any problems, yet. Understandably, they were sad and in low spirits and he did feel pity for them. To be forced to leave their homes and the land, what did they repeatedly say, "of the grandfathers." Well, it wasn't his fault and he had a job to do and would get paid right handsomely for it too.

The long line of wagons began slowly at first, but once all of them were moving, the pace became more rapid. The wagon path was smooth and wide as this was the same path that thousands of white settlers had used for years as they had traveled across first the Alabama Territory and then the State itself.

Just before reaching the destination of the frontier town of Wetumpka, two Creek men coming from the rear of the wagon train halted Ingersoll asking him to stop.

"What is the reason to stop? Is there a problem," the contractor asked, wiping the perspiration from his sunburned face with his yellow handkerchief.

"Yes, four of the wagons will not move," one of the men answered, not knowing how to explain why. The other quickly added that a long piece of metal was dangling from underneath the wagon,

Realizing that the wagon's would need to be repaired and that it would take time, Ingersoll called out to Soaring Eagle and his men, whom he now knew were his relatives, to go down the line of wagons and tell the Creek to make camp early for the night. They were also told to find one of the half-breeds that knew the way of the blacksmith to repair the wagons. He wanted them moving early the following day.

Having done what was asked of them, Soaring Eagle, Badger, Fox Slayer and Horse Stealer returned to the wagons of their families. Before they were settled, a loud commotion was heard just ahead of them as, yet another group of white men lead by a man wearing a badge and waving his pistol, loudly proclaimed that he needed to talk to the one in charge of the injuns.

"That would be me. I am Stephen Ingersoll. What can I do for you?" Ingersoll asked tersely, obviously irritated by the man.

"Well, you see," the man said, spitting tobacco juice near the feet of Ingersoll, "Some of your folks here owe money and…"

"No, all their debt was settled yesterday. They will pay no more to you and I expect that you and your men need to leave. We will be on our way first thing in the morning and you will not be bothered by them anymore," the conductor replied.

Frowning, the sheriff answered, "Well, I can get warrants for their arrest if need be. Also, I have a paper here that says that soldier man down in Florida needs some of these injuns to go down there and help bring in those Red sticks that's hiding out in the glades." Smiling with juice still running from his mouth, he continued, "Maybe if'n you pad my pockets just a little and give me three or four of these fellas to send, I'll gest leave you be."

Ingersoll was aware that the government did ask or order that some of these friendly Creeks be sent to assist General Winfield Scott in gathering the Creek and Seminole. Nodding his head and flipping a single gold coin to the disgusting man, he answered, "They will give no more money on any trumped-up charge, but I will see if any will go to Florida." Looking around for Soaring Eagle, who now seemed to be his go to man, he asked him to see if any of the Creek men would volunteer to go.

"Yes, I know of a few who expressed an interest in going to Florida. They had rather go there instead of making this trip to Indian Territory now. They will not go with this, this white man who smells of firewater," Soaring Eagle quietly said.

"No, I would not allow that. Before we leave Wetumpka tomorrow, I will have Mr. Bateman take them to the officer in charge of the U.S. Army troops there," Ingersoll said, looking intently at the tall Creek man who stood in front of him. This man obviously was or had been someone of importance. He wanted to know about him. "Soaring Eagle, after you recruit some of your men to go to Florida and have finished your evening meal, please come to my tent. I would like to talk with you."

"Yes, I will," Soaring Eagle answered as he motioned for Badger and his son and husband of his daughter to follow him. He too wanted to know about this man who would take his people from their land.

Soaring Eagle had no problem securing five young Creek warriors to go in search of the Red Sticks, knowing they would possibly join them instead of bringing them in, he quickly made his way back to the wagon of his family.

Little Flower, Little Deer and their family eagerly awaited the return of their husbands and fathers as the sun slipped below the horizon. Little Coyote had killed a large rabbit which sizzled over the fire, the aroma pleasing to the men.

"My father and my grandfather," Blue Bird screamed as the little girl ran to the out-stretched arms of her father. "We are happy to see you. Are you hungry? Can you smell the rabbit?"

"One question at a time little one," Horse Stealer said, picking up the child as he smiled at her mother.

Little Deer returned the smile of her husband and taking her daughter's hand, softly said, "Come Blue Bird, help me find the tin plates so that we may eat the rabbit that smells so good." Soaring Eagle, your face shows of your long day," Little Flower said, taking the hand of her husband. "Come, sit and rest before we eat. Can you tell us what happened to stop the wagons today?" She asked, faintly smiling. "Do the white men not want us to leave … now?"

Soaring Eagle took his wife's hand and pulled her close to him. "Oh, my Flower, he whispered, "I will tell you later when I return. I have been asked to come to the tent of Mr. Ingersoll when I finish my meal." Turning to his family, the fatigued man forced a smile, "Come let us eat the rabbit that smells so good."

Chapter Five
I Now Understand

Soaring Eagle carefully sat on one of three little canvas and wood chairs that seemed to fold. Thinking to himself, "What a strange way to sit." "Soaring Eagle, thank you for coming," laughing, Ingersoll asked, "Would you like some coffee?"

Soaring Eagle shook his head, feeling slightly more comfortable as he watched the man before him light his pipe.

"Tell me about yourself. I have a feeling that you are an important man and that your people have much respect for you," Ingersoll said as he sat down on one of the folding chairs.

Soaring Eagle hesitated briefly before he began. "I am or was chief of the Hillabee. My town was on the upper regions of the Tallapoosa."

"You were at the Horseshoe then?" Ingersoll asked, sensing the tremendous sorrow that filled this man.

"Yes, the Great Spirit allowed me to live so that I could lead my people," pausing, Soaring Eagle slowly continued. "Lead my people to a new home far from the land where the bones of our grandfathers lay."

Both men sat in silence, one remembering the sadness of the past, the other feeling shame for the part he had and was playing in the removal of these people. Soaring Eagle and Stephen Ingersoll talked, learning more about each other as the moon rose high in the night sky.

"Soaring Eagle, I now consider you my friend," Stephen Ingersoll said as both men stood. "I understand now, and I promise I will do what I can to make this journey to your new home as easy as possible for you and your people. He extended his hand to the tall man before him and Soaring Eagle clasped the arm of his new friend.

"The way of the Creek," he said as the sorrowful call of the owl filled the air.

Ingersoll looked up, startled at the closeness of the owl. "What, why is the bird so near?" He asked with a trace of fear in his voice.

"The owl has been with us for many seasons, even before the time of the Horseshoe. We were afraid at first, then my daughter was told by a wise old woman that the owl is preparing us for troubling times ahead. My friend, I fear there will be many more of these times," Soaring Eagle softly said as he walked away from the camp of the white man. The cry of the owl became more sorrowful as he slid underneath the blanket of his wife and held her close.

Chapter Six
Silver Cross and White Beads

The Creek people were up and moving early the following morning. Conductor Ingersoll had convinced Chief Opothle Yahola that the Tuckabatchee people would be able to move faster and make better time if unnecessary baggage, some of their clothing, bedding, furniture and their farming utensils were stored in a warehouse in Wetumpka. These items then would be placed on a steamboat and would be waiting for them when they arrived in Indian Territory. With much reluctance, they had agreed. The wife and daughter of Opothle Yahola had shed tears as their personal prized items had been taken from them and placed in wooden crates. Fox Slayer had tried to comfort his wife, telling her that it was better to leave the items for now in order to make a faster journey.

"Fox Slayer," she had said as tears slid down her beautiful face. "I feel that we will never get our clothing and other things back." Little Dove had been correct, as all of the personal items that had belonged to the Tuckabatchee people would rot on a steamboat in route to Indian Territory.

The Creek people passed through the town of Wetumpka supposedly without incident or problems. Several white women stood in the doorway of the small cabins and watched as the procession of wagons filled with women and children slowly rolled past. Most of them felt pity for these people who were being forced from their homes and land that they themselves now lived on. One woman, a tear slipping from her wrinkled, weathered face, went inside and returned with a large loaf of freshly baked bread. Just as the wagon of Little Flower passed in front of her cabin, the woman called out. "Stop, please, I, I have something for you. My name is Maggie and, and I am sorry that you must leave. Please take this bread. I just baked it this morning," the woman said as Little Flower stepped down from the wagon.

Dance With the Spirits

Seeing the sincerity in her face, Little Flower took the bread and smiled. "Thank you, my family will eat this bread for our midday meal." The eyes of the two women locked and a bond formed between them.

Taking a deep breath, Maggie began. "My, my son was killed over twenty years ago when we came down here from North Carolina. Some Injuns did it." The old woman stopped, again wiping a tear from her face. "I hated all of you. This has been heavy on my heart and I know that I was wrong. I prayed to my God to take my hatred away and now when I see what has happened to your people..." stopping again, the tears now freely falling, she continued. "That hatred is gone. I am sorry." Taking a strand of worn twine from her neck, a small silver cross sparkling in the sunlight, Maggie smiled at Little Flower. "Please accept this token of my forgiveness and for the hate I felt, and now for your great loss."

Little Flower smiled at the old woman, taking a string of white beads from her neck. "My name is Little Flower. I lost my father at the Battle of the Horseshoe. The life of my family had been hard and now we will leave the land of our grandmothers. I would like to give you these beads as a bond of friendship so that a part of me will remain here." Taking the twine from the woman, Little Flower handed her the beads. "And a part of you will go with me."

"Thank you, Little Flower," Maggie said. "I pray that you and all your people will find happiness in the new land. And please remember, I am sorry."

The two women clasped hands as a shout came from the front of the line of wagons for them to start moving.

Chapter Seven
White Man Mischief

The next three days were uneventful as the wagons slowly moved and Stephen Ingersoll had hopes that he would have no more trouble from either the Creek or the spiteful white men who always seemed to show up. The early September sun beat down on his face as he paused, drinking lukewarm water from his canteen. He saw his new friend Soaring Eagle along with Badger and Horse Stealer riding toward the front of the line. He had decided it best for the three of them to patrol the wagon train by riding back and forth along the long line making sure there were no problems. From the look on Soaring Eagles face Ingersoll knew that his hopes were about to be dashed.

"Soaring Eagle, what is wrong? What is the problem?" Ingersoll called out.

Frowning, Soaring Eagle answered. "My friend, blankets and saddles as well as six horses were taken from wagons near the end of the line. Two white men were spotted leading the horses away and there is more." Soaring Eagle paused, shaking his head. "Before we left the town of Wetumpka, some of my people visited a grog store and purchased fire water from the white men who were happy to supply them with all they wanted. Many of the Creek men were made crazy by the whiskey. Sadly, one man shot his own brother. I was told that he has walked the path to the Great Spirit. I do not know how to stop this behavior," Soaring Eagle finished sadly.

"And I do not know how to stop the actions of the white men," Ingersoll answered. "For many years these men have wanted the land of your people. Now that they have it, many of them plot to find ways to keep them here. They sell them whisky when it is against the law. They falsely accuse them of stealing when it is the white man who takes from the Creek people." Pausing, despair obvious in his face, he continued. "Soaring Eagle, we will work together. I will help protect the

Creek people from these unscrupulous men who thrive to continue to make their money by deceit. I will get your people safely to Indian Territory, somehow."

"Mr. Ingersoll," Soaring Eagle began.

"Stephen," Ingersoll corrected. Soaring Eagle, my name is Stephen to you. I have a feeling that we will spend much time together before our journey is over."

Soaring Eagle smiled, "Yes, Stephen, I agree." Becoming serious again, he continued. "I have talked with Chief Opothle Yahola and the lesser chiefs. They would like a military presence to guard the camps during the time of darkness. It seems this is the time of mischief by our people and the white man."

Shaking his head in agreement, Ingersoll answered, "Yes, I think this might help. I will speak with Bateman about this and see if he can arrange for several infantry to guard the camps at night. Thank you, Soaring Eagle. Go now to the family of the man who has died and make sure they do not need for anything."

Chapter Eight
I Am Thirsty

By the end of the first week of travel, the long line of Creek wagons had entered unfamiliar territory. Just as they had in the town of Wetumpka, the white women and children lined the small streets of Centerville, most of them waving as the wagons filled with Creek women and children passed by. Soaring Eagle, along with Badger and Horse Stealer had not been confronted with any new problems and the wagons continued their normal pace, some days making better time than others. They would soon be in the large white man town of Tuscaloosa.

No rain had fallen, and the hot Alabama sun had parched the ground. The small streams in the area were all but dry and the wooden barrels hanging on the side of the wagons were almost empty. The Creek people were beginning to suffer from lack of water.

"My mother, I am thirsty," Blue Bird the daughter of Little Deer and Horse Stealer said in a small voice. "May I please have some water," she asked, "My throat is very dry."

Little Deer looked closely at her daughter. She seemed to have lost weight since the journey began and was quieter than usual. "My little Bird, are you not feeling well? Does anything hurt you," the concerned mother asked as she touched the child's face and scooped the last of the water from the barrel. "Here, drink this slowly. There is no more."

Morning Star had heard the conversation between her older sister and Blue Bird. She quickly moved closer to the little girl and reached for her hand. "Blue Bird, would you like to go for a walk with me? I need to check on the family of Turtle Boy."

Blue Bird finished the water and gave the cup back to her mother, then took the hand of Morning Star. Both Little Deer and Little Flower knew that Morning Star could spend time with the child and would know if she had a sickness. Morning

Star, now approaching her seventeenth season had been blessed by the Great Spirit with the natural ability to help and heal. She had also gained much knowledge from her grandmother, Sunflower Woman and the wise old woman Sunugee. She was considered to be a beloved woman and was both revered and even feared by all who knew her.

"My mother, we will return soon. I will also look for water that runs from the ground. Do not be concerned for us," Morning Star said, smiling.

Morning Star and Blue Bird walked hand in hand back down the dusty road filled with wagons. The movement of the wagons creating a constant whirl of sand and dust. The little girl seemed to have a difficult time breathing. "Little Bird," using the name her family called her, Morning Star began. "Is it hard for you to breathe?"

Shaking her head, the little girl answered softly, "Yes, and I'm always thirsty. I hope we can find water that runs from the ground," she finished smiling, "soon."

Smiling back at the daughter of her sister, Morning Star said, "I think that we will, but first let us stop at the wagon of Turtle Boy. He can go with us to look for water. Would you like that?" Morning Star already recognized that something was indeed wrong with the child.

After securing permission from the mother of Turtle Boy, Morning Star and the children veered off the roadbed and soon found themselves in a wooded glade. Sunlight dappled through the leaves, making beautiful patterns on the forest floor. Morning Star asked the children to be silent, and soon over the late season song of the redbird, she heard the sound of gurgling water. Smiling, she followed the sound and soon saw water running from the rocks into a clear pool. She pulled a leaf from a palmetto bush and scooped to fill the makeshift cup with water. Morning Star froze when she saw the large cottonmouth only inches from her hand. The venomous snake, instead of striking, slowly slithered away. Rising with water for both children she smiled and said, "Here Blue Bird, Turtle Boy, drink this. We will then go back to the wagons to spread the word for everyone to stop and fill their water barrels. I think there is plenty."

In a frightened voice, Turtle Boy asked, "The snake, why did it not bite you?"

"Morning Star has special power. She has no fear of snakes. They will not bite her," Blue Bird replied as she drank the much-needed water.

Morning Star smiled again, but suddenly became solemn as she stopped to pull bear grass that grew around the pool of water. She knew the child would need this medicine soon.

Chapter Nine
We Will Soon Leave Alabama

Soaring Eagle and Badger had tried unsuccessfully to prevent the Creek men from visiting the whiskey filled grog shops that lined the packed-dirt streets of Tuscaloosa. The sun had not yet reached the mid-point in the brilliant blue sky when word reached them that many men were drunk and behaving unruly. Frowning in disappointment, Stephen Ingersoll, on being told of the situation, ordered the wagons to halt. He knew that several of the wagons needed repair and the women had asked to stop to wash their clothing in a small stream near the Warrior River. He hoped the Creek men would become sober before the new day because he would like to get an early start to make up for today's delay.

The new day only brought more disappointment, as the skies opened, and heavy rain fell for several hours. The Creek men not only had not sobered but became more intoxicated and were less manageable. It was only when the rain had stopped, and the men had slept off the effects of the whiskey that the wagons could move again.

Making good time, the Creek travelers reached the little village of Lexington by mid-September. They had been on the road for just over two weeks and had traveled further than Ingersoll had expected. Soaring Eagle had reported that several families were complaining of sickness which seemed to be increasing. He had not mentioned that little Blue Bird, the daughter of Little Deer and Horse Stealer was not well. Soaring Eagle was becoming very concerned for his granddaughter.

The next few days were uneventful and the wagon train and those following along on horseback continued making good time, as much as twelve to fourteen miles each day. Spirits were good as they passed through the County of Marion and on into Franklin County where the temperature reached a scorching ninety-six degrees.

The situation rapidly changed when the Creek people reached the town of Tuscumbia. Many Indian ponies had become lame, their feet cut and bruised by the small rocks that covered the roadway. To make matters worse, the Creek men had again secured the firewater of the white man and were intoxicated and lagging behind. Contractor Ingersoll was relieved when he saw Soaring Eagle and his men riding toward him. "Soaring Eagle," the contractor called out, "I need to talk with you. Come, let us ride to that group of trees over there and get out of the sun."

Soaring Eagle nodded as he, Badger, Horse Stealer and Fox Slayer rode toward the trees.

"How is it back down the line," Ingersoll asked as he slid from his horse. "Are the men still drunk?"

"Yes, Stephen," Soaring Eagle answered. "Many are bad drunk. I think it best to leave them alone. The women and children need to rest."

"We will stop for the day then," Ingersoll said in agreement. "There is another, small problem. I have no meat rations. Your people will need to make do with beans and cornmeal for a few days. I am sorry."

"We have made do with less, Stephen," Soaring Eagle replied with a faint smile. "Some of the young boys can hunt for rabbits. They will enjoy that."

"One more thing, Soaring Eagle," Ingersoll added. "I am not sure if you are aware of this or not," pausing the man looked into the eyes of his new friend, "We soon will leave Alabama and move into the State of Mississippi."

A dark shadow seemed to cross over the still handsome face of the former Hillabee Chief. Not being familiar with the territory, he had not realized they had traveled so far and were about to leave Alabama. Ingersoll watched as sadness and pain filled the man.

"I did not know," Soaring Eagle begin, "We will pass the word to halt for the remainder of the day. I will then go to be with my family."

Chapter Ten
Hard Times and Sadness

Soaring Eagle gathered his family and led them to a nearby grove of trees that provided shade from the hot midday sun. A small stream rippled over rocks, making soothing sounds. Soaring Eagle took the hand of his wife and sat down in front of his family, the sadness evident in his dark eyes. "My family," he began emotionally. "Tonight, will be our last in the home of our people. The land where the bones of our grandfathers lie," he paused, taking a deep breath, "We will leave our Alabama home behind. We have experienced much happiness and also sadness here. I remember the time of my youth," pausing again to look lovingly at his wife. "When I pulled Little Flower from the rushing stream in our Hillabee village and later watched her dance, oh, so gracefully, round and round. I knew I would never love another." With a far away look in his eyes, Soaring Eagle continued slowly, "And then the time of the owl and the battle at the Horseshoe where so many of our brave warriors would take the path of the Great Spirit. I remember feeling the sword of the white soldier enter my stomach and waking to find my wife and children gone along with all the other women and children." Tears began to slide down the strong face of Soaring Eagle as he looked at his family. "I searched, going all the way to the River of Flowering Rocks before I found them...with Badger. My friend, I would gladly have killed you that day."

Badger smiled at his friend. "I know," he admitted. "Were it not for Horse Stealer, you would have. You had every right. I have already confessed to you that I loved your wife and your children and was ready to give them a home. I thought that you no longer lived. Little Flower knew that you did."

The eyes of Soaring Eagle and Badger locked. Both men knew what had been said was true. A deep bond had formed between the two and both knew now that each would give their life for the other. Little Flower looked at her husband and then at Badger. She wiped tears from her eyes as she too remembered the difficult, sad times as well as the happiness the three of them had shared. She thought of her mother, Sunflower Women, who had been the backbone of her family and of the strength and courage that she had provided. Little Flower remembered the day of their forced removal from the Hillabee Town and how her mother had said she would not go, that her bones would lie in the land of the grandmothers. She remembered vividly her mother clutching the red beads that had belonged to her father as she fell to the ground and breathed her last.

"I am glad my mother will remain here," Little Flower said softly, suddenly feeling her presence. "I know her spirit will always be with us."

"Yes, it will," Soaring Eagle said, feeling a new sense of strength as well. "My family, we will make the best of the situation that lies before us. May the Great Spirit guide us and help us to find happiness in our new home."

Soaring Eagle again looked at his family, Little Flower, Little Deer, Horse Stealer, Coyote, Blue Bird and Badger. He knew that his son, Fox Slayer, was with Chief Opothle Yahola and his family. Where was Morning Star? She had been with them earlier. A ray of sunlight filtered through the trees shinning directly on the young maiden. Morning Star was sitting on a large rock up the path from her family. She seemed to be in deep thought, but her father realized she was again communing with the grandmothers.

Seeing her father, she smiled. "My father, the Great Spirit has heard you. He will guide us to our new home. We will find happiness," she paused, her tone becoming sad, "But we will have many hard times and great sadness to endure."

Chapter Eleven
I will Take Her Flowers

The ponies and wagons filled with Creek people entered the State of Mississippi on the twenty-fifth day of September in the year 1836. The roads had been bad and many who walked had sore feet and all were tired. When they camped by Yellow Creek, a group of Chickasaws, with much firewater were camping nearby and they were happy to share with the Creek. Many again, became drunk. Ingersoll, despite the intoxication of the Creek men, had the group quickly moving, traveling the desired twelve to fourteen miles each day. They reached the State of Tennessee on the twenty-eighth day of September.

The month of October begin with disgruntled dispositions and much unhappiness among the Creek and the men once again visited the grog shops. Conductor Ingersoll had asked Soaring Eagle to meet him at his camp after checking on his people. Soaring Eagle smiled again as he sat on the folding wood and cloth chair that he obviously found very uncomfortable.

"Stephen, why do you white men sit on this," Soaring Eagle asked. "It is much more comfortable just to sit on the ground."

"I agree," Stephen answered chuckling, "But it is more difficult to get up from the ground. Thank you for coming to talk with me. I know you had rather be with your family. How are they doing? I hope all is well, at least as well as it can be under these circumstances."

"My family, as are all Creek people, are strong and we will persevere. I have noticed more sickness in the last few days." Soaring Eagle paused, a look of concern covering his face. "The young child of my daughter, Blue Bird, is one of the sick. We do not know what the sickness is."

"I am sorry Soaring Eagle," Ingersoll replied, seeing the fatigue in the eyes of this man that he genuinely liked. "I will send Doctor Bussy to check on your granddaughter. He has also relayed to me the increase in sickness among the people. He seems to think the old and very young are extremely tired and they are not getting enough sleep. Also, the emotional strain is a factor and he did not rule out the possibility of being exposed to, what do you people say, a disease of the white man?"

Soaring Eagle nodded. He too liked the man opposite him. "Thank you. I think my Little Bird is more than tired. My youngest daughter, Morning Star, who is considered a medicine woman," he smiled, "has just seen her seventeenth summer, has been watching Blue Bird very closely. Not being familiar with the area, she cannot find the medicines she needs in the forest."

Nodding, Ingersoll added, "I truly hope the child is better soon Soaring Eagle. We will be in the big town of Memphis in a day or two. I need for you and your men to try to keep your people away from the grog shops. We do not have time to wait while they sober up. We are making good time, but any delay will cause us problems. The weather will not continue to be good and we still have far to go."

"We will try, Stephen," Soaring Eagle answered, "I am tired now and must go to my family. I hope Coyote was true with his bow and arrow today. I would like meat with my beans," Soaring Eagle said as he stiffly rose from the chair that folded.

"Oh, one more thing," Ingersoll said, "I will receive meat rations for your people when we reach Memphis. Everyone can have meat then."

Soaring Eagle jumped on his brown and white pony and quickly returned down the line of wagons, the smell of baking bread filling the air. He smiled when he saw Little Flower turning a rabbit that hung from sticks over the fire, the smell making him aware of how hungry he was.

"My Flower," Soaring Eagle called out as he slid from his horse and then held his wife close for a brief moment. "I see we will have rabbit with our meal."

"Yes," Little Flower said, smiling sweetly at the man she had loved for so many seasons. "Thanks to Coyote, who killed two large rabbits today. He has gone now to take the other one to a family with sickness, three or four wagons behind us. I am so proud of him. I know he will make a fine warrior one day." The beautiful but now mature woman stopped, "Will our people be allowed to have warriors in this land where we are going?"

Badger and Horse Stealer, hearing the question, looked at each other. "Yes," Horse Stealer answered passionately. "The white man cannot take that away from us. We will continue to live as we always have. We will have warriors!"

Badger, older and wiser than Horse Stealer, looked at the man that he considered a younger brother, "We can try to maintain our ways and continue to live as Creek people, but my brother, they will change us. They are afraid of us and our way of life. Many white people still think that we are savages, ready to scalp and brutally murder all of them."

Fox Slayer, the twin brother of Little Deer and son-in-law of Chief Opothle Yaholo, walked from the nearby wagon of his family, hearing the conversation of Badger and Horse Stealer. Laughing at their remarks he added, "And we are considered by them to be one of the five civilized tribes." Becoming serious, he continued, "I have heard talk of some of the people who already live in this land called Indian Territory. Some are like us, but many are still savages and will kill not only white men, but also the Creek. They will not like new people coming to the land they consider their own."

Badger nodded in agreement, "I have heard this talk as well. The white fathers in Washington City do not understand that all Red Men are not the same. There will be trouble."

The three friends, along with the family of Soaring Eagle and Little Flower sat by the fire eating the bread made from ground corn, dried beans and the roasted rabbit. Little Blue Bird seemed to be feeling better and had eaten a small amount of rabbit.

Dance With the Spirits

Looking up at her family, Blue Bird declared that she intended to ride with her grandfather on his pony the following day. "I want to see that nice old woman three wagons behind us. She has not been feeling well and I can take her some pretty flowers that grow along the trail. That will help her to be better."

The family sat by the fire, talking of the past and the uncertainty of the future. Soaring Eagle reminded them of the courage of the grandfathers and the strength of the grandmothers. As the family each retired for the time of rest, the distant call of the owl filled the night, becoming louder as Brother Moon rose in the sky.

Chapter Twelve
Sweet Song of the Blue Bird

Little Flower sat by the fire, rocking back and forth, keening as the grandmothers before her had done in their time of mourning. The dark night sky slowly became pale gray as the redbird began his early morning song. A song that would cheer no one on this day. Soaring Eagle stared into the flickering fire as Horse Stealer held Little Deer, tears streaming from their eyes. Coyote had walked off into the darkness. Morning Star and Badger quietly stood in the shadows. Morning Star had been the first to know. She had awakened with a terrible sense of dread. "Blue Bird, oh no, my little Blue Bird." Going immediately to the wagon where the little girl slept, she knew the child no longer lived.

Badger waited until the first rays of pink showed in the eastern sky before going to tell Ingersoll what had happened. He sent Morning Star down the long line of wagons to check on others that were sick. He feared what she would find.

Tapping softly on the tent, Badger waited for a response from Ingersoll.

"Yes."

"Mr. Ingersoll, I am Badger. I have very sad news to relay to you from the family of Soaring Eagle," Badger said as the man opened the tent flap. "The young child of his daughter has taken the trail to the Great Spirit," Badger said softly.

"I am so sorry to hear this," Ingersoll replied as he buttoned his shirt. "When did this occur?"

"During the time of darkness, she seemed to be better as we ate our evening meal," Badger said, his voice breaking, "She was such a sweet child."

Remembering the report of much sickness, Ingersoll asked if he had heard of other deaths.

"Not yet. I have sent Morning Star to check on the others we know who are sick," Badger answered. "I must go back to my family now. They are suffering much."

"Thank you for informing me. Please tell Soaring Eagle that I will come to see him when I make ready for the day," Ingersoll answered wondering at the connection between this man and the family of Soaring Eagle. "And tell him we will not move today in order for his family to, uh…take care of things."

Little Blue Bird and the others were buried in the old way of the Creek. Two old oak trees shaded seven stone-covered graves on the hillside near the roadway. Dr. Bussy had tried to save the three old men, the two older women, the little boy who had just seen eight-summer seasons but there was nothing he could do for Blue Bird. The old doctor from Tallassee had known the men and the families of the children. He was not certain what the sickness was, but he hoped it had run its course, for now anyway.

Little Deer and Little Flower sat by the grave of Blue Bird, both seemed to be in a trance. Slowly, Little Deer began the old chant of the grandmothers she had heard many times from her grandmother Sunflower Woman.

Morning Star stood behind her mother and sister, tightly holding the green stone given to her by Badger. She could feel the power of the stone. "My mother and my sister," she began slowly, her own eyes swollen as tears ran down her cheeks. "It is time for us to go now."

Little Deer shook her head, "I cannot go. I cannot leave my child here alone."

Little Flower held her daughter close as the grieving mother gave in to her pinned up emotions. "My mother," Little Deer sobbed, "why did the Great Spirit allow this to happen? My Little Bird was a joy to everyone."

"The Great Spirit is in control. He knows what is best. We should not question him," Morning Star said quietly. "My sister, she will not be alone. The Spirit of the Grandmothers have already welcomed Little Bird. We will leave a part of us here, but we must continue. Come." Morning Star took the hand of her older sister and her mother.

"Wait," Little Deer begged as she removed a small strand of tiny blue beads from her apron pocket and draped them over the rocks. Taking a deep breath, she softly whispered through her tears, "I am ready." Then touching the warm stone, she sadly added, "I will miss you my Little Bird."

The family of the little girl, Soaring Eagle and Little Flower, her father and mother, Horse Stealer and Little Deer and Coyote, along with Fox Slayer and his family, Badger and Morning Star, turned from the rock-covered grave. As they began to walk away, they heard the flutter of wings and the sweet song of the blue bird.

Chapter Thirteen
We Are Here

One by one the long wagon train filled with Creek women and younger children began moving. Many of the older men who had begun their journey walking now had joined the women. A solemn sadness covered the entire group, as each one of them had been affected in some way or the other by the deaths that had occurred. Stephen Ingersoll had offered his condolences to Soaring Eagle and his family. He had talked to Chief Opothle Yahola asking him to help refrain his people from buying whiskey when they reached the town of Memphis. He feared that the men would become more unmanageable if they were drunk. He needed to keep these people moving, hoping that movement would help relieve their sadness. He asked Barrent Dubois to visit with Soaring Eagle and his family when they stopped for the night. He knew that Barrent was well acquainted with Soaring Eagle and might be able to offer comfort to them.

Ingersoll was pleased with the conduct of many of the Creek men as they passed through Memphis, Tennessee. Some, of course, could not resist the temptation of the white man's firewater and had become very drunk. He had refused to stop the wagons, forcing the Creek men to sober on their own. As in other towns, families had stood in doorways and watched as the forlorn people passed. Again, some of the kind women had given food to the Creek women and children. Others had yelled that they were only savages and that their land should belong to the white people. The Creek people, with heads down had continued their way, glad to leave this town.

On the ninth day of October the Creek people stood in awe as they looked at the vast body of water before them. Only Opothle Yahola and only a few of his men had seen the majestic Mississippi.

"My grandfather, how will we get to the other side," Coyote asked Soaring Eagle. "I can only see water. I see no land."

The heart of Soaring Eagle had jumped with gladness to hear his grandson talk. He had said very little since the death of his sister. "Coyote," Soaring Eagle began. "Mr. Ingersoll told me that Mr. Bateman is making arrangements for all of us to board a steamboat."

"All of us? And the ponies too," the youth asked, his eyes wide as he looked back at the river in front of him. "My grandfather, I fear this journey across the grandfather of rivers."

On the thirteenth day of October, with much tribulation, over one-thousand Creek people were boarded on the steamboat Farmer and crossed the mighty Mississippi. Agent Bateman decided it best that five-hundred men should take the ponies through the Mississippi swamp. The remainder of the Creek people would go forty miles down the Mississippi to the mouth of the White River to avoid the murky swamp.

The rapid current swiftly carried the large steamboat down river as Soaring Eagle and his family held tightly to the rail. Becoming relaxed and more comfortable, they watched as large buck and timid doe peered at them from the brown and orange autumn foliage that lined the bank of the river. After the initial fear had subsided most of the Creek people where pleased and seem to enjoy their journey down the big river. Only a few of them had ever seen a steamboat and never expected to ride on one. For a brief time, the people did not think of the reason that they were on the boat and where their destination would be.

After making camp for the night, the Creek resumed their journey, reaching the mouth of the White River. Moving up the river, the travelers progressed forty-five miles before camping on the bank of the river.

Leaving before the sun rose the following day, the steamboat Farmer reached the Cashe River by nightfall. The river was extremely high and overflowing its banks, much too dangerous for the Creeks to leave the steamboat. The following day, after going back down river to a place called Rock-Roe Bluff, the Creek people were able to pitch their tents. The weather was sunny but very cold. Agent Bateman had hoped to rendezvous with the men and the ponies here, but there was no sign of either.

Having made camp at Rock-Roe in the cold and wet for two weeks, the Creek had become disagreeable. There were reports of increase of sickness, which was assumed to be Cholera. The Creek men and their ponies arrived, and Ingersoll and Bateman thought it best to move the camp immediately. Plans were made to do so on the following day.

The next few days were among the worst the Creek people had endured since leaving their Alabama homeland. The weather was cold and the roads a horrific, muddy mess. Thirty wagons had bogged down within two miles of the camp. The women and children were forced to walk in the mud, their feet wet and their clothing mud-spattered. Conditions worsened and without any comforts, many slept on the wet prairie ground. The party of Creeks were scattered for fifteen miles along the muddy roadway.

Soaring Eagle and his men assisted Dubois in getting the party of Creek together. Many were sick and the count was increasing. Despair had set in. The Creek people knew that they were in Arkansas and that there would be no turning back. This difficult situation continued for nearly the whole month of November. The Creek people cold and wet and roads nearly impassable. Little progress was made. Agent Bateman had urged the Creek people to move as winter weather was fast approaching and travel would be even more difficult. Tired of the torrents of rain and wagons stuck up to the axles in the constant mud, the Creek people were becoming discontent and cross. They were ready for this part of the journey to be over. By the end of November, the rain had stopped, and the sun had dried the ever-present mud. Enduring the cold, the Creek people were more content, traveling fourteen to sixteen miles each day.

On Thursday, the first day of December, the Creek party entered the State of Oklahoma ... Indian Territory. The Creek suffered due to the extreme cold but had continued to make good progress as they traveled through the Cherokee Nation. On Wednesday, the seventh day of December 1836, after one-hundred, nine days on a long and treacherous journey, the exhausted Creek people arrived at Fort Gibson. In wretched condition, their blankets worn and tattered, many were without shoes and they were hungry.

    Soaring Eagle and Badger were nervous as they followed Chief Opothle Yahola and the other chiefs inside the fort. "We are here," Soaring Eagle said apprehensively to Badger. "I do not know what our fate will be, but we are here."

Chapter Fourteen
The Cold Is Biting My Toes

The Creek people were instructed to make camp by a small stream near the fort. They were relieved to be able to stop and rest but were anxious about what lie ahead. Soaring Eagle and Badger had returned from the meeting with the military commander at Fort Gibson. Both looked troubled.

"My husband," Little Flower began as she placed sticks on the fire. "What words did the military man have to say? Is the news from him bad? Do they have food for us?"

Taking the hands of his wife, the tired man tried to smile. "I will tell the words of the white chief after we have our bread and beans. I am very cold," he said, stepping closer to the fire. "I long for our home on the Tallapoosa."

The weary family ate their simple meal in silence. Just as they finished, Fox Slayer and his wife, Little Dove and their son joined them. "My father and mother," Fox Slayer called out, the fatigue obvious in his voice.

"Fox Slayer, my son," Little Flower said, always happy to see him and his family. "Come, little one. Sit on my lap. Do you want some bread? We have some left over from our meal and I will put some honey on it for you." She continued as she hugged the young son of Fox Slayer and Little Dove. The little boy grinned as he hugged his grandmother.

"My mother," Little Dove said, laughing. "This child is always hungry." Pausing and becoming serious, "I guess we all are."

"My family," Soaring Eagle began, pulling his tattered blanket around his arms and moving closer to the fire. "I am glad we are all together, safe and healthy. The trip from our homeland has been long and hard. We have lost many of the old ones and the young children along the way." He looked at his daughter, Little Deer and saw the tears slide down her beautiful, sad face. "Including our precious little one, Blue Bird. She will always remain with us in our hearts." Taking a deep breath, he continued. "We are now in the place we have heard spoken of for many seasons, Indian Territory. I have heard the words from the military commander of the fort. His words were not good. He was sorry to tell us that we could not yet continue on to the land that will be our new home." Soaring Eagle paused, seeing the dismay in the faces of his family. "It seems that the white man's government does not have provisions for us and the other Creek people who will follow us. He said it could be two or three moons before we can settle on the land promised to us near the river called Canadian. We will need to camp by the Arkansas instead."

"They took our land away with the promise that we would have good land here and never again be hungry," Horse Stealer said with anger in his voice.

"My brother," Fox Slayer said to the husband of his sister. "They have tricked us again. The lips of the white man never speak the truth."

"My grandmother," a small voice broke in. "May I have more bread and honey? I am still hungry."

Breaking the tension, the child's request brought laughter to the family. "Yes, you may have more bread," Little Flower said as she rose from her place near the fire. "Please go to the other side of the wagon and bring a few little sticks from the pile to place on the fire. The cold is biting my toes."

"Can cold bite? Does it have teeth? My grandmother are you tricking me like brother rabbit?" The little boy asked with wonder in his voice.

"My, my, you are a clever one," Little Flower answered, laughing again.

"Come, my son," Little Dove said. "I will help you carry more sticks. I am cold too and I think I will also have some bread and honey."

When the two hurried off to gather the sticks, Soaring Eagle became serious again. "There is something else, the commander at the fort said that Chief Opothle Yahola will not retain his position as chief of all the Creek people. I would like for the wife of my son to hear this from her father instead of me."

"How is this possible?" Fox Slayer asked, puzzled. "Chief Opothle Yahola is our leader."

"In our old land," Badger added, "But here he will have opposition from the son and brother of McIntosh who have been in Indian Territory for many seasons."

"Here are the sticks, my grandmother," the child shouted happily. "Do you have my bread ready? Can I sit close to the fire, so that the cold does not bite my toes?"

Becoming silent when Little Dove and her son came back with the sticks, the pretty wife of Fox Slayer looked from one to the other. "What has been said that I was not intended to hear?" She asked, frowning.

"Little Dove," Fox Slayer answered. "After you have had your bread, we will go to the wagon of your father and mother. He will have words for us then. I think I would like some bread and honey too, my mother, if you have any extra. My stomach growls like a bear."

Later, after their families had retired to their own wagons, Soaring Eagle and Little Flower sat close to the fire wrapped in worn, tattered blankets. "Brother moon shines bright tonight," Little Flower said as she pulled her blanket even closer.

"Not as bright as it does over the Tallapoosa," Soaring Eagle replied, taking the hand of his wife. "My Little Flower, I do not think that I can be happy in this new land. I cannot find warmth here, not in my body and not in my heart. It is so cold."

"My Eagle," Little Flower said, searching the face of her husband. "Are you not well? Do you have some disease of the white man?"

"No, I do not have any disease. But, my Flower, in my heart, I am not well. I long to hear the rushing water of the Tallapoosa and cheerful song of the redbird and the blue," stopping short, the sad forlorn man covered his face, a face that showed of strength, but no longer of youth. "Oh, my little

Blue Bird, I miss you so."

"My Eagle, we all miss her," Little Flower said softly, realizing that Blue Bird had held a special place in his heart. "As you have said, she is with the grandmothers now."

"That is true, my Flower. You have always known what words to say. I will again one day feel the warmth of the Tallapoosa River Valley. For now, let us go into the wagon and find warmth there." As the two entered the wagon, they heard the distinct call of the owl.

"Be strong, my father and my mother," Morning Star said out loud from the shadow of the wagon. "Your family will need that strength in the seasons to come."

Chapter Fifteen
We Have Been Tricked Again

The next few days were challenging for the Creek people as they faced one obstacle after another. They were extremely disappointed that they would not be allowed to move to their new home on the Canadian River for two or three moons. Many questioned the reason given as lack of provisions. If there was no food for them on the Canadian River, how then were they going to eat on the Arkansas River? Chief Opothle Yahola had been furious at having been told that he would no longer be the head chief of the Creek people in Indian Territory. He may have been chief in Alabama, but son and brother of his old adversary, William McIntosh would have much to say about his being chief here. Rollie and Chilly and their people had been in the territory for over ten years and they were well established. The old settlers, as they were called, looked to the McIntosh as their leaders. This problem, the commander at Fort Gibson had said, would have to be dealt with and resolved between the chiefs.

When the Creek people asked for their household belongings that were promised to be waiting for them when they arrived in Indian Territory, they were sickened. "I am sorry," the commander had told them. "Due to some sort of miscommunications, all of the items that belong to you have been lost." He would not tell them that all their prized possessions had rotted or rusted on a steamboat in the Gulf of Mexico.

The Creek people under the leadership of Chief Opothle Yahola were allowed to rest near Fort Gibson for a few days. They were then told to prepare to move on to the Arkansas River where they would remain until they could go on to their permanent home.

The conditions had been unfavorable, and the Creek felt that facts had been misrepresented to them. The women who had lost their fancy blue and white china and colorful quilts for their beds had cried and the men wondered if the white

Dance With the Spirits   *51*

government would at least replace their plows that had been "lost." The Creek people were not at all happy when the wagons once again began to roll. What lie ahead for them, they did not know.

After two days of travel the Creek party, led by a raw-faced young private, held up his hand indicating that they were to stop. "This is the place I was told to bring you. You will camp here until I or other military personnel come back to lead you onward to the Canadian River. You have been provided with enough corn meal, salt meat and beans to last." He smiled. "Of course, there is plenty of fish in the river. You may even spot a deer or two to supplement your diet." Under his breath, the private muttered, "If the Osage Indians don't get them first."

Standing closest to the soldier, Badger had heard the last remark. "Private, what did you say about other Indians," he asked?

"Well yes, of course," the young man answered. "There are other tribes of your people all over the place. This is Indian Territory you know. Best watch out for the Osage. They have been known," stopping he smiled again, "to lift a few scalps. I will be seeing you. Good luck."

Soaring Eagle and Badger watched as the private and platoon of other soldiers rode back in the direction they had just come.

"My brother," Soaring Eagle said angrily, "I think once again we have been tricked by the white man. Why would they leave us here in a place that others claim? We do not know what these people will do. I do know that they will not want us here."

"I too fear for our people. We are not sufficiently armed to defend ourselves," Badger answered.
"We will alert our people to be cautious and to be on guard."

"Yes," looking up at the afternoon sky, Soaring Eagle answered, "We will need to be careful. For now, we will need to try to get our people settled before the sun sinks below the horizon. The land is flat here. I can see for such a long distance."

When Soaring Eagle and Badger returned, the stars twinkled in the night sky and Little Flower and Little Deer had the evening meal prepared. Horse Stealer had helped his wife to make camp and had been fortunate to kill a rabbit large enough to feed all the family.

When the meal had been eaten and everyone was preparing to retire for the night, Morning Star announced that she needed to commune with the grandmothers. "I will return with the morning sun," she said.

"Morning Star," Little Flower began. "I do not think you should go far from the wagon. Your father has warned us of the danger."

"My mother, I must go, you know that. I will be cautious. Do not fear for me. I will be hungry for bread with honey on the new day," the beautiful young woman said as she placed her beaded bag into the pocket of her skirt and slowly walked off into the shadows.

Chapter Sixteen
I Am Morning Star

Taking a deep breath, Morning Star reached inside her bag, touching the smooth green stone Uncle Badger had given her many seasons ago. She admitted to herself that she was more than a little afraid but as she had told her mother, she had to do this. The grandmothers were calling her. She would trust in them and the Great Spirit to protect her. Looking up at the star-filled night sky, she walked away from the long line of wagons that had been pulled into a huge circle. "Brother moon is full this night, that is good," She said out loud. Following the sound of a babbling stream, Morning Star soon found a small nook isolated by a grove of pine trees. She gathered up the brown needles from the ground and placed them beside a large rock, still warm from the afternoon sun. "This is good," She said again as she sat down by the rock and pulled her blanket around her. "I can feel the spirit of the grandmothers."

Being lulled by the sound of the stream and wind blowing through the trees, Morning Star allowed herself to fall into a trance-like state of mind. She saw the grandmothers of long ago and with them, she was delighted to see her own grandmother, Sunflower Woman. They were dancing around a fire and beckoned her to join them. Morning Star felt herself move and then join in perfect harmony with their steps. They gracefully danced round and round, their chants from a different time.

"Morning Star," She heard her grandmother say. "Tell our people to be strong and to always remember that they are of the great Muscogee." Then just as quickly as they had appeared, they were gone. The young woman rubbed her eyes, happy that the grandmothers had appeared to her. Feeling thirsty, she walked the short distance to the stream for a drink of water. Just as she cupped the cold water to her mouth, she heard voices loud in anger, coming a short distance from her.

Morning Star quietly followed the voices, seeing two young warriors in a heated argument. One of them was apparently a Creek. The other had looks that were unfamiliar.

"I said give me your coins of the white man," The unfamiliar one said. "I know you Creek have many coins."

"I have no coins," The Creek man said, honestly.

"I think that you do, and I do not mind killing you to get them. We do not want your people here. This is the land of the Osage," The other man answered angrily as he pulled a knife from his waist.

The Creek man fell to the ground as he backed away and the Osage was quickly on top of him. The two men rolled over and over with first one and then the other on top. The Osage, being larger seemed to have the advantage. He plunged the knife into the stomach of the Creek and was about to do so again when Morning Star stepped from the shadows.

"Leave him alone or you will be the one to die," She said with more courage than she felt, as she pulled out her own knife.

"Who are you? Where did you come from? "The startled man said as he jumped from the ground.

"Who I am does not matter. Leave this place, now!" Morning Star said as she pulled the wooden owl from her bag, its glass eyes shining in the moonlight.

The Osage warrior took a step toward her and stopped short when he heard the loud call of an owl. "A witch," He yelled loudly. "You are a witch. I have heard Creek people have witches and evil beings that watch over them."

The eerie call of the owl became louder. "Go," Morning Star quietly said as she held the wooden owl high for the man to see.

The Osage man picked up his knife and swiftly ran off into the darkness. Morning Star then turned back to the injured Creek man. Seeing the red that stained the front of his shirt, she knew his injuries were serious and that she would need bear grass to stop the bleeding. She quickly opened his shirt to examine the gaping wound.

"Who are you?" The Creek man asked weakly.

"I am Morning Star. I will attend to your injury. You do not need to talk," She answered.

"Morning Star, I have heard of you. Thank you for saving my life," The Creek man said as he closed his eyes.

Morning Star searched along the stream bank and was relieved to find the bear grass she needed. She cleaned the wound and then packed it with the bear grass. In case other Osage prowled the area and not wanting to call attention by building a fire, she lay down beside the man and covered them both with her tattered blanket. She prayed to the Great Spirit that this man would live to see a new day.

Chapter Seventeen
Grandmother and the Creek Stranger

Morning Star had not slept. She had listened to the sounds of the night, the different call of the hoot owl and the far-off howl of a coyote or wolf. There were also sounds she did not know in this strange land. She had watched brother moon drift brightly from one side of the night sky to the other. She had listened to the restless man beside her. She had heard his moans of pain and checked his wound often, making sure that the flow of blood had not returned. As the slightest tint of gray covered the sky and the temperature dropped, she became very cold. She checked the unknown man beside her. He was hot, very hot.

"Oh, no," Morning Star said to herself. "He has a fever. This is not good." She slipped from his side and found the bear grass, again picking up small sticks along the way and she built a small fire. Looking around, she saw the dry shell of a small turtle. "This will work," She whispered. Filling the shell with water, she added tiny pieces of bear grass and placed it on the fire. Just as the sky began to turn pink and the birds began their early morning song, the Creek man moaned loudly.

Morning Star quickly turned from the fire and rushed to his side. "I am here," She said as she touched his hot forehead. "Do not talk," she instructed. Turning back to the fire, she removed the turtle shell. Touching the liquid, making sure it was not too hot, she continued, "I need for you to drink this. Drink very slowly."

She raised the head of the Creek man, encouraging him. He opened his eyes and looked at her, then slowly began to drink. After he drank all that he could, Morning Star laid his head down and checked his stomach. The deep gash was no longer bleeding. She put fresh bear grass in the wound. The Creek man watched her and mouthed the words, "Thank You," and drifted back to sleep.

Satisfied that this man was going to live, Morning Star remembered that she told her mother she would return with the new sun. She tucked her old blanket around the Creek man and told him she would come back soon. She did not think that he heard her and seemed to be resting better than he had during the night.

When she returned to the wagon, the sun had just appeared on the horizon. Little Flower had a fire going and was preparing the morning meal. "Morning Star, my child. I was beginning to worry about you. Did you find what you were seeking?" Pausing, Little Flower looked closely at her daughter, "What is wrong? You look as if you have not slept."

"My mother, I have not slept. Yes, I saw the grandmothers," Morning Star smiled, "Including the mother of my mother. She sends words for our people."

Little Flower smiled also, wishing she had the gift of her daughter and could be allowed to see the grandmothers. "Is that why you did not sleep?" She asked. "No, after the grandmothers left me, I overheard two men auguring, a Creek man and an Osage. The Osage man stabbed the Creek and would have killed him if I…," Morning Star was interrupted by her mother, "Morning Star, did you put yourself in danger again?"

"The Osage man thought I was a witch," Morning Star laughed. "He was afraid of me when I pulled out my owl and then heard the eerie call of an owl from a nearby tree and ran off into the night."

"The Creek, what about him, will he live?" Little Flower asked as she handed her daughter a piece of bread made from dried corn.

"Yes, I will not let him make the trip to the Great Spirit," Morning Star answered. "Do we still have honey to go on my bread?"

Little Flower gave Morning Star a clay jar filled with honey. "That is all we have. I will send coyote to find a beehive and get us more. I know you are going back to him. Do you want extra bread and beans to take for yourself and the Creek man?"

Little Flower asked. "Where is he? Do you know who he is?"

"Not far from here, just over the rise near a little stream. No, I do not know his name or where he is from. That is not important. Do not be concerned for me. I will stay with him until he is strong enough to move here. But I will return before darkness covers the sky," Morning Star stated as she took the food from her mother. "I told him I would return soon."

Morning Star was soon back at the makeshift camp where she found the Creek man awake and alert. He smiled when he saw her. "I am glad you have returned," he said weakly, holding his stomach.

"Ah," Morning Star said, smiling back at him. "I see that you are awake. Let me look at you now. How do you feel?"

"I see the new sun, and that is good," He answered. "My stomach still has much pain."

Nodding, Morning Star pulled the blanket back and checked his stomach. Still raw and ugly with a slight trace of red, the wound looked better than she had hoped. "I need to put some more bear grass on the wound and then prepare more hot liquid for you to drink. I think you will soon feel better. I will go get more bear grass and rekindle the fire," She said with relief as she turned to go.

"Wait, Morning Star," the Creek man pleaded. "I know that without you, I would have taken the path to the Great Spirit. If the Osage had not killed me outright, I would have died without your help. I will be forever grateful to you."

"I am a medicine woman. It is my responsibility to help anyone in need," Morning Star answered, smiling at him. "I would like to know who you are."

"I am Hawk. My town is," He paused, "Was Autossee. The town of my grandmother was Tuckabatchee. I know of you and the many good things you have done."

"I will return with more bear grass and sticks for the fire. And when the sun is high in the sky, I will have bread for you to eat if you feel well enough," The young maiden answered embarrassed at his words.

"Do you have any honey?" Hawk asked, his dark eyes sparkling with humor.

Morning Star stayed with Hawk, attending to his wound and keeping him comfortable until the sun began to fade. He had eaten the bread Morning Star had for him and had begun to regain his strength. The two of them had talked of the difficult times and sadness their people had endured. They both feared for the future. She had told him about her being with the grandmothers and the words they had spoken. She told him the brother of her mother had been called Brown Hawk and he had walked the path of the Great Spirit at the Battle of the Horseshoe. He told her that his father had also taken the same path at the battle. He had seen only one summer then and had never known his father and that his mother had taken another husband and had died giving birth two summers later. He had lived his life with his grandmother. With tears in his eyes he said that she had come down with the disease of the white man early in their journey and that she too had walked the path of the Great Spirit. Morning Star told him of her sadness when Blue Bird, the child of her sister, had met the same fate. They sat by the fire in silence, thinking of the ones they had lost as the sun slowly began to slip behind the trees.

"I must go," Morning Star said suddenly, jumping to her feet.

"Go?" Where are you going?" Hawk asked, surprised. "Are you leaving me here alone for the night?"

"No, you are not strong enough yet. I think you will be better with the new day. Now, I am going to the camp of my mother," smiling, Morning Star continued. "We need more bread and honey. My mother and father will worry. I will return here before the first star shines in the night sky.

"Morning Star," The young man softly said. "Please hurry. I am cold and hungry. It will be good to have bread and honey," and have you close by, he thought to himself.

Chapter Eighteen
The Man Called Hawk

Morning Star had taken more bread along with the requested honey back to Hawk. She also took an extra blanket. His life was no longer in danger and it would not be necessary for her to lie beside him. She had checked the wound and was satisfied that it was healing. She insisted that he drink more of the bear grass concoction just as a precaution. They sat by the fire until darkness covered the night sky, then douched it out in fear of prowling Osage or any others who meant them harm. Her father had told her to be watchful as Osage had been sited in the area of the wagon camp.

Morning Star and Hawk sat in the moonlight, listening to the night sounds and to each other. Becoming overcome with drowsiness, Morning Star smiled at Hawk and softly said, "Hawk, I am sorry, but I must sleep. If you are strong enough when the sun shows his face on the new day, we will go to the camp of my mother."

"Morning Star, I know that you are exhausted," the young man answered. "You have taken good care of me and again I want to thank you for saving me from the path of the Great Spirit. I too need sleep."

Morning Star picked up her blanket and moved to the other side of the fire's embers. "I think we will both be warm if we lie close to the fire rocks."

"Morning Star," Hawk began, "I am cold, very cold. Please bring your blanket and lie close to me so that we can be warm. We both will sleep better." A pack of coyotes began their nighttime serenade as Morning Star laid down beside Hawk and covered them both with her blanket.

The new day dawned clear and very cold. Hawk had awakened before Morning Star and had managed to pull himself up without waking her. His stomach was very sore and tender, and he realized it had been fortunate that the knife of the

Osage man had not penetrated any deeper. In the early morning light, he looked at the still sleeping Morning Star. "She is beautiful," He said to himself.

As if she realized that he was gazing at her, Morning Star opened her eyes. "Hawk, you are sitting up. That means you are better. That is good." Quickly standing up she continued, "Let me see if there is any sign of new blood. If not, we are going," she shivered, "To find a warm fire and food. I am hungry. I know my mother will be expecting us."

It took longer for Morning Star and Hawk to reach the Creek camp than she had expected. Cold wind with fingers of ice raked through their bodies and every step caused Hawk pain as he slowly walked. Morning Star struggled to support him and was relieved to see Badger coming to meet them.

"Uncle Badger," She called out, "I am happy to see you."

"Let me help you," Badger answered, taking the other arm of Hawk.

Moving faster, Badger and Morning Star were able to help Hawk to the camp. Soaring Eagle and Little Flower met them and quickly assessed the situation. "Put him in the wagon," Little Flower said, "We need to get him warm. I will bring my blanket."

After Hawk had been comfortably settled in the wagon, Morning Star touched his flushed cheeks and then his stomach. "He is warm, and I see a slight stain of red," the young medicine woman said, turning to go. "I will return with the bear grass mixture. He is known as Hawk. My mother, please keep him comfortable."

Hawk remained in the wagon of Little Flower for two suns. The walk had weakened him and irritated the wound. He responded well to the constant care of Morning Star who left him only for short periods. Little Flower noticed how the eyes of the young man, who a few seasons ago would have been known as a warrior, lit up when her daughter came back into the wagon. She also noticed the pink on her cheek when

Morning Star looked at him. "Ah," She thought, "My Little daughter has fallen in love with this man Hawk."

Sitting by the fire, after her family had finished the evening meal and retired to their wagons, Little Flower took the hand of Soaring Eagle. She softly began talking to her husband. "My Eagle, what do you think of this young man called Hawk?"

"I think he will make a good warrior and," he paused, smiling, "A good husband for our daughter."

"You have noticed?" Little Flower asked, sliding closer to her husband.

"It is plain to see that he has feelings for her and that she feels the same for him," Soaring Eagle said reflectively. "My Flower, has our daughter seen enough summers to be a wife?"

"I remember having this same conversation about Little Deer and you asked the same question then too," Little Flower answered, laughing. "My answer is yes. We have wondered if our little beloved woman would have time in her life for a husband. I think we now know, she will."

"You are right, my Flower. Life for our people was hard and then there was much sadness when we first felt love for each other, and it continues to be so now, only in a different way. I think that Morning Star needs someone to take care of her." Soaring Eagle paused, "We will not always be here for her. Come, my Flower. Walk with me. I feel as sad on this night as the time we first heard the melancholy call of the owl so long ago."

Morning Star had heard the words of her father and mother. She had been both thrilled and saddened. Neither she nor Hawk had expressed their feelings with words to each other. Both knew it would soon happen. She had pulled her crystal from her pouch and saw a long future with this man called Hawk. She also realized that she would not always have her mother and father.

When Hawk had sufficiently recovered to leave the wagon of Little Flower, it was decided that he would stay with Badger in his lean-to, as the young man and the older one had become fast friends. Morning Star and Hawk continued to spend much time together and it became obvious that their love was becoming stronger.

Chapter Nineteen
To the Canadian

The Creek people had been camped on the Arkansas River for two moons. Rations for them were becoming scarce and the commander at Fort Gibson received word every day of their discontent at being in this temporary place. These people needed to go to their permanent home on the Canadian River.

Chief Opothle Yahola had met with Chief Rollie and Chilly, brother and son of William McIntosh. The meeting had rekindled the hard feelings between the Upper and Lower Creeks regarding an event that had happened over ten years earlier. Chief Opothle Yahola had ordered Chief Menawa along with Soaring Eagle and Badger to go to the Chattahoochee to take the life of the Lower Creek chief for the selling of Creek land to the white man. The Creek chiefs had managed to be civil and it was decided that McIntosh would remain the chief in control of the Lower Creek already established on the Arkansas River and that Chief Opothle Yahola would be the leader of the Upper Creek who would move on to the Canadian River. Eventually, the hard feelings would again return, preventing the two groups of Creek people from being completely reconciled.

Their journey would begin as soon as preparations could be made. During the time on the Arkansas River other groups of Creek from Alabama had arrived at Fort Gibson. These people had a more difficult time on their journey, most were in a destitute situation and many had not survived the trip. They too would accompany Chief Opothle Yahola to their new home.

The day of departure was cool, but sunny with a hint of upcoming warmer days. The Creek were in a good disposition with hope of getting settled and being able to plant corn and beans. Then they would not be hungry. Soaring Eagle along with Badger, Fox Slayer and Horse Stealer helped to prepare not only their family but all the Creek people for their move. They distributed the meager rations, realizing that the salt meat and corn for the bread would not last long. Their possessions were few and were loaded into wagons and the Creek families were ready to move.

Hawk, still unable to walk on his own, was helped into the wagon of Little Flower. He would guide the one remaining horse. Some families had lost both horses as many of the ponies had succumbed to the fatigue of the long journey. The raw-faced young private who had led the Creek to their first place of encampment, would again lead them to their new home on the Canadian River. Commander Armstrong had spoken to Opothle Yahola and Soaring Eagle wishing them and their people well. He had apologized for the lack of provisions and the discomfort they had endured. He assured the chief that conditions would improve when they reached their permanent home on the Canadian River. He was a God-fearing man and regretted lying to these men whom he had learned to respect. In fact, he had no idea what lie ahead for these poor destitute people.

Morning Star watched as her people readied themselves for their journey. She offered encouragement and helped everyone, stopping to check on the mother of Little Turtle who was recovering from a sickness. The young medicine woman had been very attentive to the situation around her and she listened closely to the conversations of her father. She was not at all confident that the lives of her people would improve when they arrived at their new home. As the wagons began their slow pace, Morning Star pulled the crystal from the beaded pouch that had been a gift from her friend Sinnugee so many seasons ago. When the bright light of the morning sun touched the smooth surface of the stone, the crystal immediately became streaked with red. She tried to conceal her emotions, realizing that many who had trust in her were watching. The soft sad call of the owl filled the morning air and the Creek people knew what Morning Star had seen in her crystal.

Chapter Twenty
December 2018
The Drum Beat

Shadows had begun to fall as the sun slipped into the western horizon and Minnie Raintree shivered, visibly chilled by the cool air. "My goodness, how quickly the time has flown by this afternoon," the old lady said, as she stiffly rose from her chair. "Let me see what the final score of the football game was and then I will warm us some soup. You boys rather have tomato or potato? Matthew," she smiled, her original teeth still pretty and even, "I think the sandwiches you brought would be good now."

"Yes mam," Matthew answered, "I think we would like potato."

Nodding, Minnie Raintree continued as she pushed on the TV remote, "Well then, would you boys go out to the porch and bring in some more firewood? I think we will have a frost tonight. Yea, Alabama," she yelled, heading back to the kitchen on the other side of the room.

The two boys went outside the little cabin, stopping short at the sound of yapping near the edge of the woods. "What was that?" Jacob asked, backing up.

"Think it was a coyote," Matthew answered as suddenly a chorus of howls filled the air," Don't think they will harm us, but let's get the firewood and get on back inside."

"Man, that's a weird sound, but you know what, I kinda like it," Jacob said as he picked up several pieces of firewood. "Think we can come back out later and hear more night sounds?"

"Yep," Matthew laughed, "I thought you would like it out here. Now let's go back inside. I'm hungry and Aunt Minnie Raintree's soup smells good."

The boys and Minnie Raintree rapidly consumed the stack of sandwiches and the big bowls of steaming-hot potato soup that had been laced with cheese.

"That was delicious Aunt Minnie Raintree," Matthew said, wiping his mouth on the brightly colored napkin.

"Yes, it was," Jacob added, eying another plate of chocolate chip cookies on the counter. "Aunt Minnie Raintree, do you suppose that I could have one of those cookies?"

Laughing at the young man, Minnie Raintree answered, "Of course, you can have two if you like. Go get the plater and share them with me and Matthew. We do need to save some for later tonight when we have more hot chocolate. Soon as I clear the dishes, we can continue with our story. I am enjoying this so much!"

"We are too, Aunt Minnie Raintree," Matthew happily answered. "Can we help you in anyway?"

"No, well yes you can. We will need more wood for the fire tonight. There is a big stack out by the little storage shed near the woods. It will save having to go out later if you would go get it now." Looking out the window she continued, "My, its already black dark. I don't like these short days. I always have so much to do. Here, take the flashlight."

"Yes, mam, Jacob wanted to hear more of the night sounds, anyway. We may stay out for a few minutes, "Matthew said.

"Better get your jackets then, its already cold out there," Minnie Raintree laughed. "You will hear night sounds alright," She paused, "If you listen closely, you may hear the drums."

Matthew and Jacob exchanged looks as they went out the door. "Drums, did she say drums?" Jacob asked. "What is she talking about?"

"I'm not sure, but maybe we'll find out," Matthew replied as he turned the flashlight on bright and walked toward the edge of the yard to the shed.

Only hearing the silence of night and the soft flow of the river at first, the two young men thought they would not hear the night sounds at all. Suddenly the pack of coyotes began their chorus of howls only to be answered by another group from across the river. A barred owl delivered a loud session of hoots, obviously disturbed by the presence of the two young men.

"Let's take the wood to the porch and sit on the steps," Matthew said quietly, not wanting Jacob to know that he was a little unnerved to be so far from the light of the cabin.

"Sounds like a good idea to me, too," Jacob laughed softly.

Sitting down on the steps Matthew turned the flashlight off. Both were still and silent. They waited only minutes before hearing a chilling scream and then another and another.

"Think I've heard enough," Jacob said with fear in his voice. "Let's go inside."

Minnie Raintree had quietly opened the door and sat down by Matthew. "That was a bobcat. Have lots of those down here. If it is not cornered, it won't hurt you. I think we should stay out for a few more minutes. There is more you should hear."

Strangely, both young men were calmed by Minnie Raintree's voice. "Sounds like a woman screaming," Matthew proclaimed.

"Yes, it does. Let's be very quiet now," Minnie Raintree said.

The sound was very low and seemed to be coming from far away, and then the drumbeat was unmistakable. Matthew and Jacob both gasped as Minnie Raintree pointed to a spot in the old cotton field. Shadowy figures were dancing in unison around a fire that only moments before was not there. Matthew rubbed his eyes. "Oh, my! Is this real or am I dreaming?"

"I'm having the same dream if you are," Jacob said weakly. As quickly as the figures had appeared, they were gone, and the beat of the drum was silent.

"Let's go in now," Minnie Raintree said with a quiver in her own voice.

"What did we just see Aunt Minnie Raintree?" Matthew asked softly, "How was that possible?"

The old woman had tears running down her cheeks when she turned to look at the young men. "I am so glad they came tonight for you to see. Matthew my boy, I don't understand it

Dance With the Spirits 71

either. Those were the Spirits of our ancestors, of Soaring Eagle, Little Flower and Morning Star. Come, now let's go in and get comfortable by the fire, there is more of their story to tell."

Chapter Twenty-One
The Spirit Will Be with Us

Matthew placed another log on the fire and Minnie Raintree brought three fuzzy throws from a shelf in her bedroom, handing one to each young man. "Now then, let's get comfortable and I will begin," Minnie Raintree said.

"Aunt Minnie Raintree," Matthew began hesitantly, "about, what we saw. Did we really see Soaring Eagle or are we…"?

"Matthew, my boy, sometimes, it is best not to question what we do not understand. The Spirit of my people is strong, and they are very real. I feel great honor that they came to us tonight," the old woman paused, her dark eyes twinkling with tears. "I think it best that this remains a secret between the three of us, do not tell anyone, understand?"

Both boys nodded. "Yes, mam," Matthew replied, "We are ready for you to tell us more. Did Morning Star and Hawk get married?"

"Yes, they did. Such a sweet ceremony. I will tell you of that a little later. My people had hoped that the hard, sad times would be over when they reached their new home on the Canadian River. They were wrong, very wrong," Minnie Raintree said sadly.

* * * * * * * *

With the lack of enough ponies to pull the wagons, more time and effort was taken to make the journey to the Canadian River. The young private and the small group of soldiers who had guided the Creek had tried to help but there was very little that could be done. The soldiers felt pity for these poor destitute people. What would become of them? How could they survive?

Chief Opothle Yahola and Soaring Eagle led the Creek past village after village of different tribes of people. Those who had arrived earlier from Alabama and Mississippi, even the Osage and others who had always lived on the western side of the big river. Many watched them pass in silence while others waved cheerfully.

"There are so many," Opothle Yahola said. "Where will we find the land promised us? Is there any that is left?"

Soaring Eagle shook his head. "I have never seen so many people, even in the towns of the white man."

The Creek travelers continued, following the Army Private until there were no more people and the land became desolate and isolated. The private turned in his saddle and waved his arm. "Chief, here is your land, the place where you will build your new homes."

Opothle Yahola and Soaring Eagle exchanged glances. "There must be some mistake," Opothle Yahola exclaimed in disbelief. "We were promised good land with plenty of water where we could plant our corn and never want for food again,"

The private shrugged his shoulders, "I am sorry," He said. "This is where I was told to bring you."

Opothle Yahola placed his hand on his knife, but quickly removed it when Soaring Eagle shook his head. The private pretended not to see the actions, not wanting to create anymore problems for the chief or his people. "Chief Opothle Yahola," the private began, "I am truly sorry. I know this is unfair for you and for all your people. I am also sorry to tell you," He paused again, "that the provision wagon only contains enough food to last a few days. I do not know what you will do after that."

Dejected and tired, the formerly flamboyant chief looked across the barren land in front of him and then at the wide shallow river. "We expected nothing more from the White Father in Washington. We know from experience that he speaks with a forked tongue. My people will survive." Turning to Soaring Eagle, Opothle Yahola continued, "At least there is a river, it is not the Tallapoosa, but a river. Come let us go and help settle our people. The morning sun will bring a new day and a new beginning for the Creek people. Again, I say, we will survive. The Spirit of the grandfathers will always be with us."

Chapter Twenty-Two
Corn from the Horses

The days and months that followed continued to bring hardship and sorrow for the Creek people. They had been forced to leave their ancestral home in Alabama to come to this unfamiliar, hostile land, and were promised better than this. The plows and hoes that had been lost because of governmental negligence had not been replaced. Lacking the farming implements created difficulty in planting. Many, many were hungry. The old and the young once again succumbed to the diseases of the white race. The white man, with their whiskey, continued to plague the Creek men and often the Creek women as well. Many of them had no resistance and would spend their precious few coins on fire water. This, along with discontent and misery created behavior problems among the people. Their situation was dismal. Some of the more industrious had immediately searched for food sources and felled trees to build cabins for their families. They would rely on the Spirit of the grandfathers and the Giver of Breath to see them through this difficult time.

Little Flower, using the hoe fashioned in the way of the grandmothers, was busy clearing weeds from around her small garden. She was glad she had remembered to bring corn and bean seeds from her Alabama home. They at least had this. Stopping to wipe sweat from her face, she smiled as she saw Soaring Eagle approaching, her heart beating faster. The seasons have aged him she thought, noticing the strands of gray in his hair. "My Eagle," she called out. "Were you able to catch any fish for our evening meal?"

Smiling back at his wife, thinking she was as beautiful as she had been in her youth, Soaring Eagle answered, "Yes, but only two. Come back with me to our," He smiled again, "cabin." The cabin only partially completed, was better than most and would do for the warm months. He continued, "I have had words with Opothle Yahola, and he wishes for me and Badger to travel back to Fort Gibson. The commander informed us he would have more rations for our people by this time. You know how badly we need food. Also, Opothle Yahola gave me coins to purchase corn if necessary. I would like for you to travel with us. We will leave with the new sun."

"I will go with you Soaring Eagle," Little Flower answered puzzled, "But why do you wish for me to go?"

"You have been working hard to provide food for not only our family but also," Soaring Eagle smiled again at his wife, "I know what you do to help others. I think you need a time to rest."

Soaring Eagle, Little Flower and Badger left before the new sun and made much better time than they had on their journey to the Canadian River a few moons ago. They again passed by the many settlements and villages of others and again they were starred at almost threateningly by some, while others offered them food and wanted to know how the Creek people fared.

Camping by a small stream, they enjoyed the bread of corn that Little Flower had baked the day before. Soaring Eagle and Badger loved each other as brothers knowing that each one would die for the other. Badger had also loved Little Flower for many, many seasons and he would do so until he followed the path to the Great Spirit. Soaring Eagle knew too that Badger could be trusted completely. The three talked of days long ago, the times of sadness and heartache after the Battle at the Horseshoe. The time when Badger took Little Flower, her children and mother along with many other women and children to his home on the Chattahoochee River. And of how Soaring Eagle had vowed to follow them to edge of the big waters to find his family. They laughed at the antics of the children and how now they had children of their own. Tears came to the eyes of Little Flower when they talked of Blue Bird, the child of Little Deer who had walked the path to the Great Spirit much too soon. And finally, they marveled at the gift of Morning Star and Badger declared she would do much for her people in future times of hardship.

Brother moon had risen high in the night sky when they gave in to their fatigue of travel. Little Flower slept in the arms of Soaring Eagle and Badger watched from across the fire, pushing away his thoughts of love for her.

They reached Fort Gibson before the sun set the following day. Commander Arbuckle was happy to see Soaring Eagle and Badger and thought to himself how beautiful Little Flower continued to be. He asked them to join him for the evening meal. Soaring Eagle refused the invitation asking only for bread and beans. They would not sit at the table of a white officer and eat his fine food while their people were starving. Arbuckle nodded, understanding the pride and devotion this man had. He agreed to meet with them the following day.

At the appointed time, Soaring Eagle and Badger met with the commander. Little Flower, having seen other Indian women walking around the Fort grounds, decided she would remain outside. She told Soaring Eagle that she had no business in the meeting with the white leader of the fort.

Little Flower sat on a wooden bench outside the office of the commander. She watched, more than a little intimidated as men and women of all colors, white, red and black walked from place to place. Many of the Indians were of different tribes and she had no idea what the words where they spoke. Most passed her by unnoticed, but some of the soldiers nodded at her as they walked by, wondering who she was and being struck by the beauty of the older woman.

She noticed that several soldiers were feeding their horses and that much of the corn had carelessly been allowed to fall to the ground. When the soldiers mounted their horses and rode away, piles of corn remained. As if by instinct of the grandmothers, Little Flower stood, removed her apron and walked to the pile of corn. Bending, she began scooping the yellow kernels into her apron. Passing soldiers stopped and looked at her.

"What are you doing?" One of them asked.

"Horses were eating that corn," Another soldier added.

Little Flower looked up at the soldiers and softly answered, "Corn left from the mouths of horses can feed my people who have nothing. Our old ones and children are hungry and some no longer live. I will take this corn so that others may not meet the same fate."

An old Indian woman had heard the words of Little Flower. She too removed her apron and helped pick up the corn. "For your people," She said sadly.

Coming from the office of commander Arbuckle, Soaring Eagle and Badger saw the actions of Little Flower. Both were filled with pride. It mattered not to her that she would face ridicule, her people were hungry. To her surprise, several soldiers and more of the Indians that had crowded around told her that they too would bring more food for her people. Commander Arbuckle had told Soaring Eagle and Badger that provision wagons would be sent out the following day for the Upper Creek people. Corn and beans had already been purchased from the Lower Creek on the Arkansas River and he promised that the pork would not be riddled with worms. Soaring Eagle, Badger and Little Flower would return to their home with not only aprons full of corn, but wagons of food. This had been a good day.

Chapter Twenty-Three
Dream of the Grandmothers

Soaring Eagle, Little Flower and their family, Fox Slayer, Little Dove and their son, Horse Stealer, Little Deer and Coyote along with Morning Star, Badger and Hawk had just finished their evening meal. Coyote had again killed two large rabbits, the first in many moons and the women had gathered beans and squash from the small field they had worked together. Badger had traded for some early season peaches that Little Flower had dried and sweetened with honey. The pleasant sounds of early evening had begun, and the family sat in silence, each reflecting on the hardships they had endured and survived. Five moons had passed since their arrival and while this was not home and they were not happy or even content and still did not have enough to eat, they were becoming accustomed to the territory in which they now live.

Morning Star, in her soft yet commanding voice, was the first to break the silence. "The grandmothers appeared to me in a dream." Her family immediately turned to look at the young woman who seemed to have a special glow about her.

"The words they had for me offer encouragement for our people. The sad times for us will continue," She paused, a look of sorrow covering her face, "for many seasons. There will be times that are good and then hardships will return, again and again. The grandmothers tell us never to forget that we are of the great Muscogee and that we should seek the guidance of the Giver of Breath and that we will survive." Morning Star paused again and smiled, "The grandmothers also say that we should have the Green Corn Ceremony again, that our people need that time of renewal and acceptance now that we are in this new land. They want us to find happiness again and," She smiled and took the hand of Hawk who had been by her side. "My grandmother, Sunflower Woman had special words for me. She said it was time for me to take Hawk as my husband and this should be done in the old way of the Creek at the time of the Green Corn Ceremony."

Soaring Eagle hugged his daughter and happily replied, "The grandmothers are wise. We will celebrate the Green Corn Ceremony in two moons, and we will also have a Creek wedding celebration. This will bring happiness to our people."

"Yes," Little Flower added, "Our people need a reason to be happy again and this makes me very happy."

Later, when all their family had returned to their cabins and Morning Star and Hawk had taken a walk under the bright light of brother moon, Soaring Eagle and Little Flower sat and talked by the dying fire embers. "My Flower, the power our daughter has in communicating with the grandmothers is frightening to me. I do not understand her ability to do this," Soaring Eagle said as he pulled his wife closer to him.

"We have known since she was a young child that she had special power. We should not question what we do not understand," Little Flower answered looking puzzled.

"What is wrong, Flower," Soaring Eagle asked, seeing the strange look on her face.

"I do not know. I feel that these are words of the future and will be spoken by someone yet unknown to me," She replied.

"They are good words, my Flower," Soaring Eagle answered his wife. "Come, let us go into our cabin now. Brother moon is high in the sky and I am tired."

Chapter Twenty-Four
Green Corn Again

Much preparation had been put into the upcoming ceremony, mainly in securing enough food for the many people who would attend. The men, who no longer considered themselves warriors, and the older boys had gone far from their homes on the Canadian River in search of deer and a strange-looking animal the white man called an antelope. The women had baked bread using anything they could find to add flavor, from occasional nuts to wild berries. The corn crop, the main source of food of the Green Corn Ceremony, had been small and only token amounts were available. The Canadian River did teem with fish and the younger boys did their part by catching many.

The traditional cleaning of the square ground and the discarding of old utensils and replacing them with new would certainly not be necessary or practical. There were no new to replace the old. Regardless of the changes, there was much excitement about the Green Corn Ceremony which would begin with the new sun. Unlike in times of old, before the white man had changed the way of life for the Creek people, this ceremony would only last for two days instead of six or eight. Day one, would begin with talks of the chiefs and older men. There would be very little talk from the old ones, so few remained. The much-anticipated dances would begin in the evening after the food was consumed and would last long into the night. The celebration would continue on the second day and would culminate with the wedding ceremony celebration of Morning Star and Hawk.

Hawk had already done as Creek tradition required, partially building a small cabin and had fortunately been able to kill a deer for their food. Morning Star had baked bread and prepared beans and squash. Everything was ready for the celebration and for the Green Corn Ceremony to begin. This would be the first such ceremony in two seasons and no marriage celebration had been held by the Creek people since their arrival in Indian Territory.

The new day dawned clear and warm and hundreds of Creek people came from up and down the Canadian River. Many from other tribes that lived near the Creek also came, all bearing their contributions of various kinds of food, some varieties unknown to the Creek.

Opothle Yahola smiled as he saw the mass of people before him, feeling for an instant that he was back home on the Tallapoosa. "My Creek people and my new friends," he began, "Welcome to Tuckabatchee Town. Today we will begin a time of renewal for our people. For two seasons," he paused, "No, many more than that, our people have suffered greatly, and we have lost many of our old ones and the young. We are here now in this new land, a land the white man has chosen for us. I, like you, am not happy with the situation we find ourselves in, but my hands are tied. I can do nothing."

Opothle Yahola had not had the opportunity to talk to his people all together for many moons. He took advantage of the time he had now, promising them that their lives would be better in the future. They would have to be, he had said, as he did not think they could be any worse. He had ended his talk, as always, by reminding them that Creek people would persevere, and he hoped that everyone would enjoy the celebration of Green Corn today and the wedding celebration the following day. The crowd around him cheered when he said, "It is time to eat." The combined food that the people had contributed had strangely been enough to fill the stomach of everyone, even with some left for the following day.

A large fire had been built in the makeshift square ground and the dancing began. First with the shabbily dressed women, who seemed to be embarrassed both by their attire and their lack of rhythm. Afterall, it had been more than two seasons since they had last danced. Slowly, as the drumbeat tempo increased, the women too began to enjoy themselves and happily glided around the fire just as they had done in the days of old.

When the women had finished, the men took their turn around the fire. Unlike the women, they danced with enthusiasm, as if they were releasing their pent-up emotions. Knives flashed in the fire light as the men went around and round. After the men danced and had rested briefly it was time for them to dance with their women.

Soaring Eagle had taken the hand of Little Flower and they slowly danced around the fire with others following them. The men held their wives close as the drum beat slowly came to an end. Brother moon was high in the night sky as the resident Creek retired to their cabins and the visitors went to their camps. Morning Star and Hawk had sat discreetly out of sight and watched the dance. They would have their day with the new sun, and they were the only ones to hear the far-off call of the owl.

Chapter Twenty-Five
A Dream

Morning Star quietly closed the wooden door to the cabin of her mother. She had awakened before the first rays of the morning sun and knew the grandmothers called her. As she walked the new path to her favorite place in the woods, she felt joy in hearing the early song of the redbird. She knew this would be a beautiful day for herself and Hawk. She sat on a large rock and leaned against an old pine tree, listening to the gurgle of the small stream and closed her eyes, soon drifting into a trance. Hearing a faraway sound of drums, she felt herself in a different place and a different time. Morning Star saw her mother and father in their youth standing before a large group of Creek people. An old medicine man, who she knew was Wolf Fella, was speaking in the old tongue of the Creek. She watched as her father kissed her mother and she realized she had just witnessed the wedding ceremony of her parents.

The beat of the drum became louder. She heard the sound of muskets being fired and the big boom of the cannon. She heard screams of the injured and dying and saw Creek warriors falling to the ground. Morning Star saw the father of her mother as he fell after being hit by a musket ball in the back. The child he had been carrying pinned beneath his bloody body. She saw her father cry out in sorrow as the brother of her mother fell at his side and then cry out in agony as his own body was pierced with a sword and the pain of the butt of a musket crashing down on his head. Tears fell from the eyes of Morning Star as she vividly saw the Battle of the Horseshoe.

The young woman covered her ears as the sorrowful call of the owl became louder and louder and then faded away. She saw her grandmother Sunflower Woman and her mother and brother along with hundreds of women and children being herded away like cattle. A warrior treated them kindly and refused to let the others harm them. It was Badger. He took them far away to a strange place beside a river with flowered rocks underneath the shallow water.

Morning Star saw her father near death, his only thought was to survive and find his wife and children. The power of Wolf Fella, the wise old medicine man, had prevented him from taking the path to the Great Spirit. She watched as her father traveled for many moons in search of his family. She saw the struggle between her father and Badger when he found his wife innocently in the arms of the warrior. She knew her father, Soaring Eagle would have killed Badger if the future husband of her older sister had not intervened. She watched as the two men learned to respect each other and the great bond that formed between them. She understood now the relationship between her father and mother and Badger.

Morning Star heard her name called softly and turned to see her grandmother, Sunflower Woman standing before her. "My grandmother, you are here." Morning Star answered.

"Only to you, my child. I want you to know our story so that it may be passed on to others who will come after us. I wanted you to know firsthand of the great trials of our family. You and our people will continue to face many trials and much sorrow. It will be your responsibility and honor to help our people. You, with the support of Hawk will make a difference in the lives of many. Go now, my child, back to your present time. It is a time for great happiness for you and the beginning of a new life filled with joy and many children."

"Grandmother, wait, tell me what I am to do?" Morning Star said out loud, opening her eyes, only to see no one. The young woman then realized that her grandmother had appeared to her in a dream, a dream that was very real.

Chapter Twenty-Six
The Wedding Celebration

The stunned young maiden slowly walked back to the cabin of her mother. Little Flower stood outside by the fire, slowly stirring sofkee in a big, black kettle and was not surprised to see her daughter come from the wooded area near their home.

"Morning Star, good morning, how," Little Flower stopped short when she saw the expression on the face of her daughter. "My child, what is wrong? What have you seen?" She asked, guessing that the grandmothers had appeared.

"My mother," Morning Star said smiling, "How beautiful you were on the day of the wedding celebration for you and my father."

"What? How do you know that?" Little Flower asked confused.

"Mother, grandmother Sunflower Woman allowed me to see back into the past. I saw the day of your wedding celebration. I was at the Horseshoe. Oh, mother, what a terrible time. I saw Badger take you to his town and how my father found you. I know you would have loved Badger if my father had not returned, but you knew that he lived and would come for you." Morning Star paused and hugged her mother. "My mother, grandmother Sunflower Woman then came to me. She said she wanted me to know these things so that I may pass them on to others. She said we will again have many trials and much sorrow." Smiling she continued, "My mother, she said that me and Hawk would have great happiness and many children, and I will help our people."

A little unnerved by these words, Little Flower answered, "I do not understand these things, but I am so happy for you. "Here," Little Flower filled a bowl with steaming sofkee and gave it to Morning Star. "You have a big day ahead and you do not need to be hungry. Soon it will be time for us to make you beautiful for your wedding celebration."

"I think she's already beautiful," Soaring Eagle said in a strong voice as he came from the cabin, "Almost as beautiful as her mother was on our day of celebration."

"I agree that she is already beautiful," Badger added, coming up the path from his cabin. Hawk, behind Badger, with the light of love in his eyes agreed, "She could not be any more beautiful."

The five of them ate their morning meal and Little Flower quickly shooed the men away, telling them that she and Morning Star had much work to do before the wedding celebration began. Little Flower had wisely saved and prepared a deer hide from many seasons' past. She and Little Deer, the older sister of Morning Star, had painstakingly made a beautiful dress and trimmed it with tiny white beads that had also been saved from long ago. Morning Star would need to be barefoot during the celebration as there had not been enough deer hide to make new moccasins.

The large crowd of Creek and those from other tribes had assembled around the square ground. As they had done the day before, all brought their contributions of whatever food was available. The Creek people were eager for the time of celebration and the renewal of spirit. All of them had put the time of sorrow away and wanted to see the celebration ceremony of Morning Star and Hawk. Many of them knew of her power to commune with the grandmothers and of her healing ability. Some were even afraid of this beautiful young woman.

Tears slid from the eyes of Little Flower as her daughter stood before her. "My child, you are beautiful," pausing she pulled a string of tiny blue beads from her pouch. "These belonged to grandmother Sunflower Woman, she would want you to have them."

Morning Star bent her head for her mother to place the beads around her neck and looked into her small mirror. "My mother, I look as you did on the wedding celebration of you and my father."

"Now, time has come into a full circle. Your grandmother

wore these on her wedding celebration also," Little Flower said as they heard the sharp rap of the drum indicating it was almost time to begin. "No, not yet, my mother, I feel that others will wear these beads, just as grandmother Sunflower Woman and you and now I will," Morning Star softly said as she kissed the check of her mother. "It is time for me to go to the square ground." She opened the cabin door and looked out, "Oh, mother, there are so many people."

"Yes, our people wanted to be involved in the celebration for you and Hawk. Come," Little Flower said, taking the hand of her daughter.

Another rap of the drum silenced the excited crowd. Little Flower led Morning Star to the edge of the square ground and whispered to her daughter that she loved her and then turned to join Soaring Eagle and Badger along with the others of their family.

Morning Star was strikingly beautiful. Her dress fit her slim body perfectly. The blue beads hanging gracefully around her neck was a reminder of a different time. A time when the Creek people were happy, and their lives were good. Many noticed her bare feet and thought this only added to the simple beauty of the young woman.

Hawk, quite handsome himself, appeared from the crowd and joined Morning Star. Someone began playing a soft melody on a flute and the two joined hands and walked to the center of the square ground.

Chief Opothle Yahola stepped forward, never missing an opportunity to speak to a crowd of his people. He began in a slow, distinct voice, "Welcome my people and friends. We are happy that you have joined us this day for the wedding celebration of Hawk and Morning Star. It is their desire to have a traditional Creek ceremony in the old way of our people. The necessary things have already been performed, so join me now in wishing Hawk and Morning Star much happiness." He laughed and continued, "And may the Great Spirit of the people grant them many children to fill their cabin." Pausing,

Dance With the Spirits

Opothle Yahola became serious. "This is the first wedding celebration to be held in this new place where we now live. I pray to the Great Spirit that this is the first of many, so that our people can replenish and survive. May this union of Hawk and Morning Star be a new beginning for the Creek people. Let us now celebrate."

Hawk turned to Morning Star and softly whispered, "I love you my beautiful shining star. I promise to take care of you until I walk the path of the Great Spirit."

Opothle Yahola turned to the couple and tenderly kissed Morning Star on her blushed cheek and clasped the arm of Hawk in the way of old. The large crowd erupted in cheers, many of the women keening as tears fell from their sorrowful eyes that now saw happiness in the two young people before them. Considered to be a good omen, a red tail hawk flew over the square ground and a blue bird sang its cheerful song. No one heard the sad far away call of the owl, no one except Morning Star.

Again, there was food for everyone. As it had been in celebrations of the past, a few of the Creek men had brought their fire water. There was much talk and laughter and then the dancing continued long after the sun had slipped into the horizon and brother moon was high in the sky. Visitors from the other tribes were invited to join in the celebration and both groups were able to forget the sad, difficult times they had experienced, for a brief period, anyway.

The celebration continued as Hawk and Morning Star had discretely slipped away. They prayed to the Great Spirit for a long, happy life together and for their people to again find happiness in this new land that was far from their Alabama home.

Soaring Eagle and Little Flower had smiled as the young couple walked away from the celebration, remembering that they had done the same so many seasons ago. After they had greeted many old friends from Tuckabatchee and also new ones they had met along the way, Soaring Eagle took the hand of Little Flower and whispered, "Come."

Leaving the joyful sounds of the celebration behind, they walked down the moonlit path to the Canadian River. They listened to the soft sound of the flowing water, neither speaking until they heard the distant cry of the owl. "The owl, it has followed us here," Little Flower said sadly.

"Yes but remember what our daughter told us so long ago. The owl is preparing us for what is to come. It is not bringing misfortune to us," Soaring Eagle said, turning his wife to face him and tenderly kissing her. "Oh, my Flower, we have had many good times and so much sorrow. I love you so."

Little Flower looked at her husband and saw tears sparkling in his dark eyes. "Soaring Eagle, my Eagle, is something troubling you? We should be happy on this day," Little Flower stated with concern.

"I do not know. I do not understand my feelings. I am happy for our daughter who is no longer our child but the wife of Hawk." He paused, looking out at the river. "This is not our river. Little Flower, I want to see the Tallapoosa. We are going home."

Chapter Twenty-Seven
December 2018
Hot Chocolate and Cookies

Minnie Raintree yawned and stiffly rose from her chair. "Boys, I think it is time for some hot chocolate and cookies. While I get that ready, would y'all please bring in more firewood," Minnie Raintree smiled, "Now don't stay out too long. It's very cold out there."

"Aunt Minnie Raintree, you aren't too tired to continue, are you?" Matthew questioned as he and Jacob fastened their jackets.

"I am tired, but we can go on for a while longer," the little old lady said. "There is still much more to tell, but remember we still have the morning."

"Yes, mam," Matthew said laughing. "Jacob and I will be back in a few minutes and we will be ready for that hot chocolate."

The boys stood on the small porch and listened to the night sounds as they had earlier. It wasn't long before the bone-chilling cry of the bobcat filled the air and a chorus of coyotes began yapping while the bard owl hooted from deeper in the woods.

"I could get use to this," Jacob said softly, "I hope we can come back to see Aunt Minnie Raintree. So, you think we will hear the drums again?"

"I don't know," Matthew answered as he picked up a few sticks of firewood. "Maybe we were meant to hear the drum and see," he paused, "what we saw."

The boys stood outside for a few minutes longer until they both were shivering and then went inside. Minnie Raintree had huge cups filled with steaming hot chocolate and another plate of even larger cookies. "Aunt Minnie Raintree, where did the cookies come from?" Matthew asked. "I thought we ate all of them earlier."

Minnie Raintree smiled at her great nephew of whom she had become very fond. "Matthew, my boy, one can never have enough cookies, especially if they are chocolate. Now before we continue with our story," she paused, "You know it is more than just a story, it is the legacy of our people, one that has been passed down for generations. Now, I am passing it on to you." Minnie Raintree became emotional, tears forming in her dark brown eyes, "And you must promise to pass it on. The story must not ever die, if it does, the spirit of those who lived long before us will also die." Wiping the tears that had slid down her wrinkled but still pretty face, she continued. "Now, what was I going to say? Oh yes, before we begin, go to the closet near the door and get the sleeping bags and two blankets. Then y'all will be set for sleeping later."

Minnie Raintree settled back down in her favorite chair by the fire and the boys sat on the slightly worn, but brightly colored Indian-print sofa. "Let me see," Minnie Raintree said. "Where did we leave off? Oh yes, Soaring Eagle had just told Little Flower that they were going home."

"Aunt Minnie Raintree," Matthew began, "Did Soaring Eagle and Little Flower really come back here to the Tallapoosa?"

"Oh yes," Minnie Raintree answered excitedly, "Remember, he said that he would come back. It took a little longer than he had hoped, but he did come back here to the Tallapoosa."

Chapter Twenty-Eight
1842
We Will Make Plans

Five seasons had passed since the wedding celebration of Hawk and Morning Star. As grandmother Sunflower Woman had predicted the couple were happy and content. Morning Star had given birth too soon to a tiny baby girl in the time of the first cold season after their ceremony. The baby was buried underneath a tall red oak tree that stood on a hill overlooking the river. The hillside was filled with stone-covered graves, both young and the old who had walked the path of the Great Spirit. Morning Star had gazed into her crystal and she had heard the sadness of the owl's cry. She had known her baby would not live.

Morning Star spent much time helping others in their times of need. Many of the Creek people called on her if they were without food or if they were in pain or in their times of sadness. They often called on her to predict the outcome of situations of uncertainty. They depended on her wisdom and strength to get them through whatever problem arose. She was indeed their Beloved Woman.

The Creek had continued to endure difficult times in the five years they had been in Indian Territory. Often, there was not enough food to prevent them from being hungry. There were times when the government of the white man did not provide what was promised and times when the corn crop was bad. As it had been for decades, the white trader still beat them in trade, but they had very little to trade now. White men also continued to temp the Creek men and the women with fire water.

Chief Opothle Yahola had requested teachers for the white children to come teach the Creek boys and girls. Also, he had asked for the preachers from white churches to come speak to his people. Many were opposed to this action, considering it an invasion of Creek culture and their lifestyle. Other accepted the outsiders, somewhat, thinking as Opothle Yahola did, that the Creek could better deal with the white man if they understood him better. No one wanted to be like the whites and had no intention of changing from the Creek men and women they were. Morning Star realized this might not always be true.

The grandmothers still appeared to her, but not as often as before. Morning Star feared that the time would come when they would not. In the most recent visit, they told her that soon the white government would tell the Creek people that they could have no more Green Corn Ceremonies or dance in their savage ways. The white preachers, the grandmothers had said, would tell them they were the children of God, not some Great Spirit. They would not listen when the Creek people would try to explain that the Great Spirit was their God and that the Great Spirit and the God of the white man were the same.

Little Flower smiled as she watched the twin boys of Morning Star play with bow and arrows that Badger had made for them. The four-year-old boys were full of energy but well-behaved children and created much excitement for the family. Little Flower who was approaching her sixtieth season of life, enjoyed watching them while Morning Star performed her duties as Beloved Woman.

"My grandmother, come quick," Young Eagle yelled out, "I shot a bird with my bow and arrow."

"No, I shot the bird," Spotted Hawk responded louder. The twins had been named for their grandfather and father and only Morning Star could tell them apart. Young Eagle wore an eagle feather in his hair while Spotted Hawk wore the feather of a hawk. At times the mischievous boys would exchange feathers, confusing even their mother.

"Look," Little Flower answered the twins, "I see two arrows. I think you both hit the bird. Now, you will need to prepare the bird so that I can make stew for our midday meal."

Looking at each other, the boys answered in unison, "We do not know how to do this."

"It is time for you to learn. This is not just a bird. It is called a grouse and when I add corn and beans and make the stew it will be enough for all our family to eat. Come, let us get busy. Grandfather Soaring Eagle will be proud," Little Flower said happily.

There were days when Little Flower was content. She still missed her Alabama home and Soaring Eagle talked about going back. He said the opportunity and time would come. For now, Little Flower had her family to care for. Little Deer and Horse Stealer had not had more children after they lost Blue Bird on their journey. Their son Coyote was a handsome young man with many maidens competing for his attention. Fox Slayer and the daughter of Opothle Yahola, Little Dove had their son and a daughter. Then there was Badger, whom Little Flower had hoped would find someone to love overtime, even though he had told her long ago that he would never love again. He was a permanent fixture in their family and loved each one as if they were his own.

Little Flower showed the twins the art of preparing the grouse. They had been eager to learn and had enjoyed smearing blood on each other's face. This saddened Little Flower that these children would not know many things that Creek boys had experienced in the past. She had laughed as they dotted her checks with their red fingers and vowed that her grandchildren would know the way of the Creek, somehow.

The grouse stew had been tasty and was enough for all of Little Flowers' family. They had set by the fire and talked of old times in the Creek Nation back home. They had laughed at the humorous ones and then cried over the sad. The twin boys had climbed onto the lap of Soaring Eagle, begging him to tell of the times of war when he was chief, and their uncle was a great warrior.

Later, after everyone had returned to their own cabins, Soaring Eagle had held Little Flower close. "My Flower," he whispered, "Your husband is becoming one of the old ones and I may walk the path to the Great Spirit before many more seasons pass. I do not want to be here in this land when that time comes."

"Soaring Eagle, you are not one of the old ones," Little Flower cried out. "Do not speak of walking the path."

Soaring Eagle silenced her by kissing her tenderly. "I will soon see my sixty-second warm season. I am no longer a young man. I have talked with a new arrival from our old home. He tells me that some of our people are going back. Like me, they will not stay in this place. He also brings word from my friend, Trader Walker near Tuckabatchee Town. Trader Walker said he will allow me and my family to live on his land. He will protect us from the white government by allowing us to help work his fields of corn and the new crop called cotton. My Flower, we would be as the black man, but we would be home on the Tallapoosa."

"My Eagle, are you serious? Do you mean this, that we will go back?" Little Flower asked softly. "Will the government of the white man allow us to go?"

Soaring Eagle smiled at his wife. "We will not ask if we can. We will just go. Others are doing this."

"When? How soon, my husband? Will we take our family with us and…" Little Flower excitedly questioned?

Laughing now at his wife, Soaring Eagle answered, "This is good. I am glad you are happy. We will go as soon as plans are made, and the time is right. We will take our family with us if they too want to go home. For now, I am ready to sleep. Come my wife, with the new day, we will begin our plans."

Chapter Twenty-Nine
Time to Go Home

Soaring Eagle had told Little Flower to save back all the food she could. He had talked with his family and only Fox Slayer had said that because of his family connection with Opothle Yahola, he would stay for now, but he too would return home to the Tallapoosa eventually.

Soaring Eagle wanted to leave in the late warm season in order to be back in Alabama before the time of cold began. He had told only a few of his closest friends of his plans, realizing it best to keep this quiet. He had talked with Chief Opothle Yahola, who had been disappointed with his decision to go back. He had understood, telling Soaring Eagle that he too wanted to go but could not. The two old friends who had been through so much together clasped arms, with the chief wishing Soaring Eagle safe travel and success in his return trip back home.

Morning Star had looked deep into the crystal and was happy to see only the sparkling stone with no streaks of red that she had seen in the past. She had talked with many of the people who had depended on her power and strength and explained to them that it was the will of the Great Spirit for her to go. Others would step up to take her place here. Many had shed tears at her words, but realized she knew what was best and prayed for her well-being, wishing they too had the courage to go.

They would need only one wagon for the women and children as the men would ride their horses. All the supplies they needed were packed and personal items were again stored in the same trunks they had used on their journey to Indian Territory. They had brought very little when they came and would take little back. Soaring Eagle and his family would leave before the new sun streaked the sky the following day. The time had come for them to go home.

Soaring Eagle, Little Flower and their family made good time. The weather was good, and they encountered no problems. When they reached the Arkansas River the ferryman did not ask why they were going in the wrong direction. He gladly accepted the gold coin that Badger gave him and took the family across. Soaring Eagle knew it was best to stay on the less-traveled roads, if possible. He had obtained a map showing the best way back to Alabama and he and Badger studied it carefully each night. He did not want to waste time or put his family in danger because he did not know where he was going. He certainly needed to avoid the white government forts and contact with soldiers.

    The family had been on the road for two weeks without facing any obstacles. Along with the food supply they had brought with them, Horse Stealer, his son Coyote along with Hawk had provided deer and rabbit and there was ample food. Everyone was happy and in good spirit. Soaring Eagle hoped to have his family back on the Tallapoosa in about half the time it had taken to make the journey to Indian Territory.

Chapter Thirty
Sweet Brown Drink

Little Flower, happily singing a song she had learned from her mother, was busy preparing the evening meal. She realized that their life would never be the same and that other family members and friends would be missed, but they would be returning to the land of the grandmothers and they would be happy.

Hawk and Coyote had become close friends, and both spent much time planning for the future and helping to provide for their family. The two came back to camp with each carrying a large grouse and laughing about how the twins had argued earlier over who had killed their first grouse.

"My grandmother," Coyote yelled. "Look! We both have grouse, but my aim was best. Little Flower laughed with her grandson, then suddenly tears began to slide down her face. "Grandmother, why are you crying?" Coyote asked startled.

"I am sorry Coyote; your words bring back memories of long ago when your uncle Fox Slayer and I competed to see who the best shot was. So much has happened, and we can never go back to the time when life was so good." Looking around, Little Flower continued, "Where are the twins? Are they not with you?"

"No, we thought they were helping you," Hawk said. "They must be with Morning Star then," he finished with a hint of alarm in his voice.

Little Flower shook her head, "Star has gone with her father and Badger into the woods in search of plants for her medicine," she answered, beginning to panic. "Horse Stealer and Little Deer went to the spring that we passed for water. Oh, where can they be? Young Eagle, Spotted Hawk," she called out, hoping the boys had climbed into the wagon and gone to sleep or were playing a mischievous trick.

Soon everyone had returned to camp. No one had seen the boys. The family searched the area thoroughly, still no sign of

Young Eagle and Spotted Hawk. Little Flower, sick with worry herself, tried to convince Morning Star and Hawk that they had just wondered off and would be found safe and unharmed.

Through tears, Morning Star hesitantly pulled her crystal from her skirt pocket and looked into the stone, fearing what she would see. She smiled and wiped the tears from her face. "My stone is clear, I see no sadness there and I can hear the happy song of the blue bird, not the sad cry of the owl. My boys are safe, and we will find them.'

The sun, still brightly shinning, had begun its decent into the western sky. Soaring Eagle frowned, "We need to find the children before darkness falls. They will not know how to take care of themselves. Little Flower, I want you, Little Deer and Morning Star to stay here in case they return. We," pointing to Hawk, Horse Stealer, Coyote and Badger, "Will spread out and search until we find them." He kissed Morning Star on the cheek and hugged Little Flower, "And we will find them."

The women sat in silence and watched as the sun slipped behind the horizon. Little Flower began singing an ancient song of the grandmothers, her daughters joining her. Little Deer built a fire and the women listened as the night sounds came to life.

A sliver of brother moon rose and provided very little light in the night sky. Little Flower and her daughters continued to wait, becoming more fearful. First one and then another put more wood on the fire and the coyotes began their nightly chorus of howls. Hearing movement in the woods, all three jumped up anticipating the return of the men with the twins. There were no children.

Soaring Eagle, with a look of despair and fear covering his face, pulled his wife and daughter to him. "It is too dark to see. We will go back out with the new sun. We will find them."

Soaring Eagle and his family sat by the fire, first in silence, then in prayer to the Great Spirit for the safe return of the twins. Little Flower again sang the songs of the grandmothers. The long night was finally over and the sky slowly began to turn pinkish gray.

Even before the first rays of the sun began to streak the eastern sky, Soaring Eagle, Hawk, Badger and Horse Stealer were preparing to go in search of the twins. Morning Star had tearfully checked her crystal again and was relieved to see nothing that would indicate sorrow. The men were about to leave when they heard voices coming from the road they had traveled earlier.

Seeing them first, Morning Star with tears streaming down her face ran to meet the twins. She grabbed both at the same time and pulled them to her. Little Flower was right behind her, closely followed by the others. The old Indian man behind the boys smiled and asked, "Boys look same, belong to you?"

"Yes, yes, they do," Soaring Eagle answered emotionally. Everyone gathered around the boys crying and talking at the same time.

The old man stood back while the family enjoyed their happy reunion with the children. When they all had hugged the boys, Soaring Eagle turned to the old Indian. "Thank you, we feared greatly for the boys," he continued softly. "I was afraid we would not see them again. Where did you find them? I am sorry, my name is Soaring Eagle and these happy ones are my family. What are you called?"

"My name Choctaw George," he smiled. "live on other side creek," he pointed toward the small stream. "Me fish on this side. Find boys, be dark soon. Not know who belong. Take home with me. Give food. Sleep, me bring back. Good boys. Happy find family."

Thank you again Choctaw George. We do not have much, but I can give you a yellow coin of the white man," Soaring Eagle said as he reached into the pouch at his waist.

"No coin," the old Choctaw answered smiling, "You have brown drink of white man?"

"We do not have any fire water," Soaring Eagle answered.

"No, fire water, sweet drink," the man proclaimed.

"He means coffee laced with honey," Little Flower explained.

"Yes, yes, coffee," He answered quickly.

"We do have coffee and we will share with you. Come," Soaring Eagle beckoned his family and the old Indian.

Soaring Eagle and Badger talked with the old Choctaw while they drank the sweet brown drink from tin cups. The men instantly became friends and exchanged their hard-luck stories of the past. "Where you go?" George asked as he stood, indicating that he had to leave, that his woman would worry for him.

"Home," Soaring Eagle answered, "Home to the Tallapoosa."

"You go Alabama?' George asked. Soaring Eagle nodded. "If Choctaw George young man, go too," he said clasping the arms of Soaring Eagle and Badger. "May Great Spirit be with you," the old Choctaw man said as he slowly walked back down the little road and was gone.

Soaring Eagle frowned. "That old man seemed familiar. I know I have talked with him before, that he has helped me in some way. He reminds me of, no, that is not possible."

"My husband," Little Flower, "Who did he remind you of?"

"He reminded me of Wolf Fella," Soaring Eagle answered.

"Morning Star, hugging her twins, whispered to her father, "There are some things you can not understand."

Chapter Thirty-One
We Will Cross Over

Not having any more problems, Soaring Eagle and his family continued to make good time. They had been successful in avoiding the main roadways of travel where occasional groups of Creek people were still making their way to Indian Territory. Soldiers and government officials also frequently traveled these roads and Soaring Eagle knew it would be difficult to explain what his plans were. He had no intention of going back to Indian Territory, no matter what. He and Badger had talked about the possible problem of crossing the grandfather of rivers, the Mississippi. They had boarded a steamboat to cross years before and arrangements had been made then by the government. It would be more difficult to arrange for horses and one wagon to cross now, especially when they were going the wrong direction. He knew others had found a way to cross and he would too.

Camping a mile or so from the big river, Soaring Eagle and Badger had ridden to the bank of the majestic Mississippi. They stared in wonder at the sight before them as the water rushed by. "I cannot see the bank on the other side," Badger said. "My brother, how will we cross?"

Taking a deep breath, Soaring Eagle answered, "I do not know, but we will."

The two men sat by the fire after eating their evening meal, both were silent and in deep thought. Morning Star had put the twins to bed in the wagon and sat down by her father. "My father, I know you are troubled by this problem of crossing the big river."

"Yes, Star, it is an obstacle. I will not give up; we will cross over."

"Father send Uncle Badger to the nearest town on the river. A town where the big boats will be. One Indian man will not be noticed. He can find out when the next boat will cross. I do not know how but we will be on that boat and we will cross.

Dance With the Spirits

Soaring Eagle looked at his daughter, "You have had a vision?"

"Yes, this will not be easy and there may be problems, but I see us on the other side," Morning Star answered as she stood. "I need to talk with the grandmothers now. Be safe Uncle Badger."

Badger left camp before the sun rose on the new day. He would do as Morning Star had suggested. He soon found himself standing on the bank of the river again. This time he was surrounded by the hustle and bustle of a big town and long wharfs. He watched in amazement as men of all colors who spoke different languages walked up and down the long planks carrying big boxes and crates. He saw a large flat boat, he thought it was called a ferry barge, anchored in the middle of the river. Realizing that Morning Star had been correct, that no one paid him attention, he moved closer to a fancy front brick building where two important-looking men were talking. "The next bunch of Indians are scheduled to arrive tomorrow. Have the ferry go over to the other side for them to board and bring them across. Then load up with cargo to be taken to the steamboat waiting over there," the man pointing across the river.

Badger smiled. "Here is our way across," he thought as he got back on his horse and headed back to camp. He told Soaring Eagle what he had heard. "This is good," Soaring Eagle said, "We will be on the ferry when it makes the trip back across."

Not having any idea when the ferry would arrive with the new group of Indians, Soaring Eagle had his family waiting on the bank of the river just out of sight of the town as the sun rose over the east bank. Morning Star had told them to speak only their native tongue in the presence of any soldier or white man and to wear their most worn clothing. They needed to appear to be the poor, ignorant people as they were considered to be by the white man.

They watched as the ferry anchored in the middle of the river began to slowly move toward the far shore. Little Flower pulled fried bread from a pouch hooked to the side of the wagon. Her family liked this new way of preparing bread and it was much quicker. They sat and ate their bread and watched the river for the ferry to arrive. When the ferry appeared, Soaring Eagle loaded the women and children on to the wagon and reminded them to speak only in Creek if they spoke at all. He also asked Morning Star to keep the boys quiet if possible.

No one seemed to notice as they made their way to the section of town where the wharfs were located. Morning Star looked at her crystal. It was clear. The flat boat ferry slowly edged closer to a wharf and Soaring Eagle moved his family closer, blending in with the multitude of other people. As the small group, maybe two-hundred or so, of frightened Indian people walked from the wide wooden ramp leading to the wharf, he motioned for his family to move the wagon and horses on to the ramp and they were swiftly on the flat boat. Suddenly a loud voice called out, "You there, stop." Soaring Eagle took a deep breath and turned around. "My orders are to deliver you people to this side of the river. You need to get off here," a suntanned weathered man shouted out over the noise.

Soaring Eagle shook his head and pointed to the other side of the river and answered in Creek, "Family there, go to them."

The man frowned, only understanding the word family which Soaring Eagle had purposely said in English. Another man with similar appearance ran up to them and shouted that the cargo should be loaded. They had orders not to waste any time. The first man looked at Soaring Eagle and his motley family and shrugged his shoulders. He reckoned the man still had family on the other side. He did not care if they went back over but it would be their problem getting back to this side. He motioned for them to move out of the way as large crates and boxes were placed all around them.

Soaring Eagle smiled as the ferry began the slow trip across the wide river. When they reached the other side, his family would be in Mississippi. They were going home.

Chapter Thirty-Two
Our People Will Not Be There

The barge slid alongside the giant steamboat and the cargo was soon loaded from one to the other. All that remained was Soaring Eagle, his family, their wagon and horses. The ferry operator looked perplexed. He could not move the barge any closer to the bank without becoming grounded. The captain of the steamboat had watched and saw the family that remained on the barge. He realized these people were attempting to go back to their home, somewhere. He was not necessarily an Indian lover, but he did not think they had been treated fairly, being forced from their homes as they had been. He would help them, he suddenly decided. He had brought the group of Indians down river that had crossed earlier so he could take this family upriver to the place where the others had boarded. Then they could reach the bank on the wharf there. The captain yelled out to the ferry operator to allow the family to board the boat and what the plan was to help. The operator waved in response glad that this problem was resolved. Soaring Eagle and his family were soon on the big boat, very similar to the one they had crossed the Mississippi on years before. They heard the belch of the steam as the boat lurched forward and the paddle wheel began to move. The captain came down from his position in the wheelhouse to talk with Soaring Eagle. There was something different about these people. He wanted to know where they were from, the place they had called home before.

"I am Captain Brown. I will take you upriver to a place where you can go ashore," he resisted the urge to extend his hand to the stately-looking Indian man.

Looking deeply into the eyes of the man, Soaring Eagle felt he could be trusted. "I am Soaring Eagle. This is my friend Badger. Thank you for your help."

"It is my pleasure to help you and your family," the captain replied. "Soaring Eagle, may I ask where you are going?"

"We are going to the Tallapoosa. Our home is in Alabama," Soaring Eagle proudly answered.

The men continued to talk and soon the whistle on the big boat announced their arrival at the point of their departure. Captain Brown concluded, "Soaring Eagle, I wish you and your family safe travel and success in returning to your Alabama home. You will need food." He turned to a deck hand and ordered him to go below and get several sacks of ground corn and beans along with salt pork for these people. As the family began to disembark, the captain extended his hand to Soaring Eagle, "So long my new friend."

Soaring Eagle thought it best to move his family on as quickly as possible. So far, there had been no opposition, and no one had tried to stop them, yet. When they camped for the night, they were already several miles from the big river. He and Badger again studied the map, still planning to avoid the big, white man towns. Soaring Eagle smiled as he watched his wife and daughter prepare their evening meal. Thanks to the kindness of Captain Brown, they had ample food and could easily add rabbit and deer to supplement the food that had been supplied. He hoped to be on the Tallapoosa before the leaves on the oak trees turned orange and red and the ground became white with frost.

The twins sat at his feet as they ate the pork and dried beans along with bread made from the ground corn. "My grandfather," Spotted Hawk said, "This meat is good. Will we have good food when we get to our new home?"

"What will our new home look like?" Brown Eagle inquired as he reached for more bread.

Soaring Eagle remembered that the boys had been born in Indian Territory and had not known about life on the Tallapoosa. "Yes, yes," he began, "The food will be good, and Alabama is beautiful. You will like it very much."

"My father," Morning Star softly said, "It has been many seasons since we have been there. Please remember that some things will have changed. Our homes will be occupied by white men and women. Their children will play where we once played. We will not be allowed to have our Green Corn Ceremony and live in the old way of our people." She paused, "My father, our people will not be there."

Soaring Eagle looked at his daughter and realized that her words were true. Shaking his head in agreement, he sat his empty tin plate down and reached for the hand of his wife. "Come, my Flower, walk with me."

The two walked a short distance from their camp and sat on a large flat rock next to the path. Brother moon had just begun to shine, and the familiar sounds of the autumn night were soothing. "My Flower, have I made a mistake? Am I wrong to take our family home?" Soaring Eagle asked with pain in his voice. "Our daughter is right. Nothing will be the same and our people will not be there. Should we go back to Indian Territory?"

"No, Soaring Eagle," Little Flower answered gently stroking his face that was no longer young. "No, you are not wrong. It was the best thing for us to do. We have accepted change before, and we will do so again. We will be happy with just our family and the new way of life we will have. When the time comes, we will walk the path to the Great Spirit and rest in peace in the land of the grandfathers. I love you Soaring Eagle. Let us go back to camp now and rest. We will soon be home."

Chapter Thirty-Three
Back Home on the Tallapoosa

Their pace was good, somedays covering close to twenty miles and Soaring Eagle and his family soon made their way across Mississippi and the tip of Tennessee. The fall weather was sunny and mild, and food was still plentiful, only running out of the tasty salt pork. Still avoiding the larger towns, not from fear of encountering government officials, but from local citizens who now considered this land their own. Even in the smaller towns they passed through more white men and women walked up and down the dusty streets or sometimes walked on wooden boards that lined the store fronts. They learned that this was called a sidewalk and was intended to keep feet dry in wet weather.

Soaring Eagle and his family were stared at as they passed through these towns, some of which did not exist on the journey to Indian Territory. For the most part the white men and women curiously watched as they passed by, only occasionally did some of the rougher-looking men yell out using their coarse vile words, "What are you dirty Injuns doing here?" At times, women as they had done before, offered them food, which was politely refused.

The family camped near what was considered the State line, a new white man term which separated one state from another. To Soaring Eagle this meant very little, but he did understand that with the new sun he and his family would be back in their homeland. They would be in Alabama.

The new day was sunny, but cool and Soaring Eagle had his family up and moving even before the sun rose over the eastern horizon. He felt a sense of elation that this journey had been successful. He prayed to the Great Spirit to continue to guide them on this last phase back home. Passing through familiar towns, Soaring Eagle became more excited and hoped to see the Tallapoosa in three or four suns. He had been somewhat surprised to see other Creek people traveling along the

Dance With the Spirits

way. This was a good sign. More of his people were coming home.

The words of Morning Star came back to him as he stood at the edge of what had been for hundreds of years the sprawling town of Tuckabatchee. A deep feeling of sadness filled his heart and tears ran down his face. Remnants of a vast cotton field was all that remained of what had been his home. Only a few small cabins dotted the edge of the field near the woods and the river. He doubted that any of his people dwelled here now. How could changes come so quickly? Morning Star touched his arm with tears in her eyes as well. "My father, we should not mourn for what is gone. The Great Spirit has allowed us to return. It was the desire of your heart. My father we will be happy and try and preserve the ways of the Creek people. That is the will of the grandmothers."

"You are wise my daughter," Soaring Eagle answered, composing himself. "I cry also in happiness for our return to the home of the grandfathers and the grandmothers. Come, let us go now in search of Trader Walker," he chuckled. "I doubt he is still a trader," he paused, "I think he owns much land that once belonged to the Creek people and now has many coins of the white man."

As Soaring Eagle and his family moved closer to the cotton field that had been the home of the Creek people, he noticed many people doing various kinds of labor in and around the fields. He saw the black man, the white man and a sight that thrilled him, he saw a few of his own people. They all stopped their chores and looked at the family of Creek. Riding closer to a white man who had been busy repairing a broken plow, Soaring Eagle pulled his horse to a stop in front of the man who eyed him suspiciously but nodded his head in greeting.

"I am Soaring Eagle, can you tell me the name of the man who now owns this land?" Soaring Eagle asked, swallowing the lump in his throat at saying the words.

"The old injun fighter Woodward owned this land. Jest sold it bout a year ago. Don't really know who owns it now, was told to jest keep work'in," the man answered. "Why you want to know anyway? What are you doing at this place now? Thought you people were gone."

"I am looking for Mister Walker" Soaring Eagle answered, ignoring the last comment of the man. "Do you know of him?"

The man pulled a soiled bandana from his pocket and wiped his face. "Well, let me see now. Yeah, think I do. Walker owns a big track of land across from the bend in the river. You know where that's at?" Smiling at the man, Soaring Eagle answered, "Yes, I do, thank you for your time."

Soaring Eagle rode back to his family with a grin on his face. "Soaring Eagle," Little Flower questioned, "Did the man tell you where to find Mister Walker? What words did he say that made you smile?"

"He asked me did I know where the big bend in the river is. That is the land that now belongs to Mister Walker," Soaring Eagle answered.

The family traveled along the path beside the slow-moving water of the Tallapoosa. Soaring Eagle frequently stopped and gazed at the river almost mesmerized by the motion. He was home. He would deal with whatever situation occurred. He was home, that was all that mattered. The family soon forded the shallow river near the big bend and crossed over to another vast area of cleared land, that like Tuckabatchee, had been covered in cotton. Again, many field hands were busy at various task. Soaring Eagle did not need to ask for instructions, he could see the big house on a slight hill that overlooked the fields. He knew this would belong to Mister Walker.

The family continued along the small roadway that led to the house. Soaring Eagle tied his horse to the wooden railing and went up the steps. "Mister Walker must have many, many coins of the white man," he thought as he looked at the brass knocker on the door. He frowned, wondering if it was meant to announce his arrival. Taking a chance, he raised the knocker and let it fall. Nodding his head at the sharp rap, he raised the knocker a second time. The door was opened by a young boy, who Soaring Eagle thought had seen eight or ten summers. "Papa, it's one of the Indians," the boy called out.

A gray-haired man with a walk of one with old bones came to the door, "Ah, Soaring Eagle," the man began in recognition. "I knew you would come."

"Mister Walker, it is good to see you," Soaring Eagle answered happily as the two men first shook hands and then clasped arms in the way of the Creek.

Looking over Soaring Eagles' shoulder, Mister Walker peered at the others. "I see you have your family. Tell them to come on in and I will have Sally, my cook, to fix'em up something to eat. Then you and I can talk."

"It would be best if they just sat on your porch. They are very dusty," smiling, Soaring Eagle continued, "And would spoil your nice chairs. Something to eat would be good. We have not stopped to eat today."

"Very well then," Walker said, turning to give Sally her instructions. After the quickly prepared meal the women rested comfortably in chairs under a huge oak tree. It wasn't long before the twins had made friends with several of the Walker grandchildren and they played happily under the tree.

Soaring Eagle along with Badger, Horse Stealer and Coyote joined Walker in the cluttered room he called his office. Walker settled back in a huge chair and puffed on his pipe. "Well, Soaring Eagle," he said, "Did you have any problems getting back here? I received you message from Barrent Dubois that you would return, and I was expecting you, but I had thought it would be sooner."

"No, we did not encounter any problems leaving. We did have to wait for the right time. My daughter reminded me that changes had occurred, and life here would be different, now. Mister Walker, I had to follow my heart. I had to return."

"Yes, you did Soaring Eagle and I am glad. I think you will be of great value to me," Walker said. The men continued to talk, and Walker told Soaring Eagle his plans. "You and your family will live on my property and work for me. You will not be my slaves. You will be free to leave anytime you wish, but as long as you are here with me, I will prevent the Alabama government from sending you back to Indian Territory. And they would, Soaring Eagle," he paused, "I have several families of Creek here with me. You remember that my wife is related to Big Warrior. Your family will be safe as long as they are here."

Soaring Eagle nodded. He liked the words he had heard. "All of my family will be safe?" he asked.

"Yes," Walker answered, "I would like for you not to be chief of the Creek that are here with me, but certainly their leader. They are lacking that," Walker said, looking at the others, "How many cabins will be needed for your family?"

"Four," Soaring Eagle answered, hoping that was not too many to ask for, "One for me and Little Flower, one for my older daughter and her husband Horse Stealer here, one for Morning Star and Hawk and maybe a small one for my friend Badger and my grandson Coyote. Looking closely at Walker, he continued, "Can that be arranged?"

"Yes, I have two new cabins side by side available now and two more can be quickly put up. Can your family make do with two for a few days?" Walker asked.

"Mister Walker," Soaring Eagle began, "My family and I have traveled many, many miles and have seen many suns from one wagon. I think this will be good, very good. When do we begin our work for you?"

"We will talk about that later, much later. For now, let me show you to your new home. I will have one of my men bring a supply of food and the other things you will need. Soaring Eagle, my friend, I am happy to have you here at home with me. Come now, I know you and your family are tired."

Chapter Thirty-Four
December 2018
Return of the Owl

Minnie Raintree yawned and stiffly rose from her chair. "Boys, that is all for me tonight. It is well past my bedtime and I am tired. Y'all need to go back out and bring in more wood for the fire. If you need anything," she laughed, "Just look for it. I will see y'all in the morning."

"Aunt Minnie Raintree," Matthew said, "We will go into town in the morning and pick up some breakfast from Mc-Donald's."

"No, you will not," Aunt Minnie Raintree replied, "I have a breakfast planned of pancakes and ham with lots of syrup and plenty of hot coffee. I like two teaspoons of sugar, how about y'all?"

Matthew laughed, "Aunt Minnie Raintree, how did you know that we would stay overnight?'

Minnie Raintree winked at Matthew. "Oh, I knew. Goodnight, y'all stay warm now."

Matthew and Jacob woke up to the smell of coffee as the first rays of the morning sun began to shine over the treetops. Aunt Minnie Raintree had tiptoed past the boys and put more wood on the fire and had started breakfast. "Good morning boys," Minnie Raintree cheerfully said from the kitchen. "Did y'all sleep well?"

"Morning, Aunt Minnie Raintree," Matthew answered, rubbing his eyes.

"What time is it?" a sleepy Jacob asked.

"Time to get up my boy," Minnie Raintree laughed. "I'll have breakfast ready in a few minutes. Hope y'all are hungry."

Matthew and Jacob were delighted with the huge stack of light brown pancakes and plate of ham. Minnie Raintree said she liked cheese with her pancakes and the boys agree that was good too.

"Aunt Minnie Raintree, "Jacob said, "Those were the best pancakes I have ever had."

"Me too, Aunt Minnie Raintree," Matthew added, "I think I would like one more cup of coffee."

"So, would I, Matthew," Aunt Minnie Raintree answered. "I'll go ahead and clean up the kitchen when we finish our coffee while y'all get ready for our new day. Oh, by the way, I think we need more wood for the fire.

Once again, the boys settled in on the sofa while Aunt Minnie Raintree neatly dressed with her blue beads hanging from her neck, sat down in her chair by the fire. This time Aunt Minnie Raintree held a worn bible in her lap. "Boys, I always start my day by reading from the word of God. Do y'all go to church?" Minnie Raintree asked."

"Not as much as we should," Matthew answered. "We both pray."

"Good, we will pray today too," Minnie Raintree answered and began to read. "I will lift up my eyes unto these hills, from whence cometh my help…" Both boys sat in silenced and listened to her steady, clear voice as she read and began to pray. "Great Spirit," she paused briefly after her prayer, "Now let's get back to our story."

"When we stopped last night, Soaring Eagle and his family were back on the Tallapoosa and Walker had welcomed them."

"Aunt Minnie Raintree," Matthew interrupted, "Explain to me again the relation between you and the family of Soaring Eagle and Mr. Walker?"

"Yes, that is important, "Minnie Raintree answered. "I think I can make it simple. Morning Star, of course, was the daughter of Soaring Eagle and Little Flower and was my great grandmother. Now, it gets a little more complicated. Stars' daughter, who was my grandmother, married the grandson of Walker. In fact, both of her daughters, who were born after they returned here to Alabama married grandsons of Walker. That's your family connection, Matthew, understand?"

Frowning, Matthew replied, "Sort of, I think. Aunt Minnie Raintree, how is your name Walker? Both your mother and you did marry, right?" Aunt Minnie Raintree smiled. "Matthew, you are a very intelligent boy, remember earlier in the story when Walker told Soaring Eagle that he could protect them if he remained with him?" Matthew nodded. Minnie Raintree continued, "My grandmother was of course a Walker and my mother married a man who was part Indian. She continued to keep the Walker name and lived on his land so that the white man would not pack her up and move her back to Indian Territory. The man I married was white. My name was Minnie Raintree Walker Harper. He and I agreed that I should use Walker also. So, there you have it," She smiled at Jacob, "Don't think I could fit you in, but you never know."

"Aunt Minnie Raintree," Matthew said as he got up and kissed her on her brown cheek, "You are really something else."

"Matthew, my boy, is that a compliment?" She asked smiling.

Both boys shook their heads. "Alright then, here we go. Walker, and most folks called him that, practically made Soaring Eagle and his family his own. He provided for them, and they of course helped on the big farm which would soon be known as a plantation. They had a good life, never wanting for anything and Soaring Eagle was called chief again by the small group of Creek who lived on Walker land and the surrounding area. And, believe it or not, quite a few either did not go west at all or like Soaring Eagle, came back. Morning Star had two daughters, which I just told you about, and Little Deer and Horse Stealer's son Coyote married a little Creek girl who lived just down river. Fox Slayer and Little Dove, the daughter of Chief Opothle Yahola, and their family made the trip to Alabama twice over the years but returned to Indian Territory. The twins were becoming strong, handsome men who preferred to be called warriors, and Badger, like Soaring Eagle had become one of the old ones. He had continued to love all the family, especially Little Flower who had aged gracefully and had maintained the family strength as her mother Sunflower Woman had done. Everything was good for Soaring Eagle and his family. They were able to continue their Creek lifestyle while adjusting to the new ways of the white man." Minnie Raintree paused and a look of sadness filled her wrinkled face. She touched the blue beads that hung from her neck. "Then about twelve years after they had been back on the Tallapoosa, the owl came again. His cry was piercing and sad and filled Soaring Eagle and his family with fear. Morning Star, still loved by many around her, looked deeply into her well-used crystal. She shed tears at what she saw, telling her family that much sadness lie ahead for them and the entire country, both for Indian people and the whites."

Chapter Thirty-Five
1858
Cemetery on the Hill

Soaring Eagle and Little Flower sat on the little porch that lined their cabin, looking out on the vast fields of cotton that once had, so long ago, been the homes of the Creek people. "So much has changed, my Flower," Soaring Eagle softly said as he took the hand of his wife. "We are now the old ones and even our children are no longer young. Do you remember the times of our youth?" He smiled and mist filled his eyes. "The day I pulled you from the raging waters of White Oak Creek and later watched you gracefully dance with the women. Oh, my Flower, I lost my heart to you that day."

"And mine to you, my Eagle. I remember it all like it was yesterday," Little Flower answered with tears in her eyes.

"Yes, and then the day at the Horseshoe, the sorrow still fills my heart. The emptiness of knowing you and the children were gone and the thrill of finding you," he paused. "And then the fear of losing you to Badger. It is good that I have loved him like my brother for so many seasons and I know when I walk the path to the Great Spirit that he will take care of you."

"My Eagle, please do not speak such words, you are not yet that old," Little Flower said, stroking his face.

"Flower, I think I have seen seventy-eight seasons," he laughed, "Many cannot say that." Becoming somber again, he continued, "I would like to see our son Fox Slayer and his family again and I would also like to make the journey back to Hillabee Town, the town of our youth. I think I will speak to Badger about this and plan a trip. Come Little Flower, walk with me to the river. I feel the need for the soothing power I always feel when we go there." As they stood on the high bank overlooking the Tallapoosa, the sad cry of the owl filled the air.

Morning Star had been disturbed when Little Flower spoke with her daughter about the conversation she had had with her father. "My mother, Morning Star began, "Has my father complained of not feeling well?"

Little Flower shook her head. "No but seems to be sad and often speaks of the past."

Morning Star pulled her crystal from her apron pocket. She refused to look at her mother and held back the tears that threatened to fall.

The following day, before the new sun, Soaring Eagle and Badger left for their journey up the Tallapoosa to Hillabee Town, their home of long ago. Morning Star again had warned her father about much change and to expect to see many white people.

Soaring Eagle and Badger planned to return in maybe two or three suns. They took their time riding up a wagon road which was near the path they had used long ago. They passed through the new white man town of Tallassee and marveled at the stone structures that dotted the riverbank just below the majestic falls. Walker had told them of how Barrent Dubois and his Creek wife Milly had obtained land on both sides of the river and built mills to grind corn by damming the river at the falls. They had become wealthy and lived in a fine log house on the east side of the river.

Continuing on the wagon road, they soon passed through the place where the O'Real brothers had operated their trading post. The little community was called Reeltown now. Soon they reached Turtle Rattler Creek. Soaring Eagle and Badger laughed at how the white people now called it the original Creek word of Saugahatchee. Badger had told Soaring Eagle of how Little Deer had slipped from the rocks and he had saved her after the Battle of the Horseshoe. They now crossed on a fine wooden bridge strong enough to hold wagons and a team of horses.

They continued up the little wagon road, passing by small farms where white owners worked side-by-side with their black field hands, their little houses dotting the hillsides. Occasionally the workers would pause and watch the two men, obviously Indians, ride by, wondering who they were and where they were going.

They veered off the roadway and made camp beside a creek near the site of old Oakfuskee Village. Little Flower had made them bread in the old way and Badger had caught a small fish from the creek and placed it over the fire on a forked stick. The two men, who were as brothers, ate their meal and talked long into the night. Both recounting their trips to Oakfuskee Town and the visits to Menawa. How could it have been so long ago? They heard the night sounds of the past and neither spoke when the chilling sound of the owl filled the quietness of the night.

The following day they entered the bustling little town called Dadeville. Men carrying their rifles and women their baskets, hurried up and down the dusty streets. They had not ridden far when they heard a man's voice call out to them, "You there, stop." Both men stopped fully expecting this order. "Who are you and what are you doing in my town," a ruddy-faced man with a Sherriff's badge dangling from his shirt yelled.

"I am called Soaring Eagle, and this is my friend, Badger. We are just passing through," Soaring Eagle replied.

The sheriff frowned, a trace of tobacco stain on his chin, "Indians don't walk the streets here anymore."

Soaring Eagle reached into his pocket and pulled out a neatly folded handwritten letter from Mr. Walker and handed it to the man. "Soaring Eagle and Badger are men employed by me. They have been sent to Goldville to pick up materials. They are trustworthy men and will harm no one. Anyone detaining them will answer to me," signed, Walker, Macon County, Alabama.

The sheriff read slowly and nodded his head, giving the note back to Soaring Eagle. "Alright then, be on your way. I think it best for you to take another route on your way back," the sheriff said shortly and walked away.

Soaring Eagle and Badger mounted their horses and quickly rode away from the town, not wanting to encounter anymore irate white men. Why did they still hate and fear them so much? The Creek people were the ones forced to leave their homes. Taking the path off the wagon road and riding for many miles, the two former warriors, after searching, found the overgrown trail that led to Hillabee Town. They stood in sadness. Soaring Eagle remembering the life he had lived there along the banks of White Oak Creek. Tears freely ran down the cheeks of the man who had been the Hillabee Chieftain. Badger watched his friend, feeling his sorrow.

"Badger, you understand why I had to come back one final time," Soaring Eagle asked, regaining his composure.

"Yes, my friend," Badger answered softly, not wanting to hear the words.

"I feel that I will travel the path to the Great Spirit soon," Soaring Eagle paused, "Badger, please watch over our Little Flower. Keep her safe and free from harm." Badger nodded, tears sliding down his face as he hugged the man he loved as a brother.

"Let us return now, Little Flower will be waiting," Soaring Eagle resolved.

Moving at a faster pace, Soaring Eagle and Badger made it back home, sooner than expected. They had not gone through the town of Dadeville and no one else had stopped them, even though they did receive questioning stars from some of the people they met. As they passed by the town of Tallassee, Soaring Eagle noticed a group of people dressed in their Sunday-go-to-meeting cloths. They were gathered on the hill above the river. No one seemed to notice as they rode closer. "Someone is being buried here. I did not know this was a cemetery," Badger whispered.

They watched as a wooden box was lowered into the grave and then covered. A white preacher said a prayer and the tearful crowd began to sing Amazing Grace. One of the bystanders, who was obviously not a close family member stepped nearer to them and tipped his hat and said, "How do?"

Soaring Eagle and Badger nodded back to the man. "Is this cemetery for white folks only," Soaring Eagle asked?

"Don't reckon, there's some Indians buried over on the back side, think they were the first to be buried here," the man answered, "Just got to have a little money afore they'll dig the grave."

"Thank you," Soaring Eagle said as he and Badger mounted their horses and continued down river to their homes.

Little Flower and the family, including Fox Slayer and Little Dove, who had come from Indian Territory by boat were delighted to see Soaring Eagle and Badger. The family enjoyed the meal Little Flower and her daughters had prepared and they talked until late in the night. As each family returned to their own homes after brother moon had risen high in the sky, they heard a flutter of wings and the sad call of the owl. Morning Star had told her brother and sister of their father's melancholy mood and that he had said he would soon walk the path.

As Soaring Eagle and Little Flower lay close and listened to the sad cry he said softly, "The owl, you know what this means."

"No, Soaring Eagle," Little Flower cried, "Please."

Soaring Eagle turned to his wife and tenderly kissed her. "I saw a man being buried today in Tallassee Town on the hill overlooking the river. Place me there. I love you my flower. We have seen much and shared much. Our life has been good. It is time for me to walk the path." He pulled Little Flower close one final time and kissed her. Then rose and went out into the night, walking to his favorite spot above the river. He felt the soothing power of the Tallapoosa one final time, then taking a deep breath, the path was open to him. Soaring Eagle was buried in the cemetery on the hill and they sang Amazing Grace.

Chapter Thirty-Six
Soldiers in Blue and Gray

The loss of Soaring Eagle was heartbreaking to everyone who knew and loved him. No one understood his prediction of his own untimely death, except Morning Star. Not only did she understand, she had known it would happen. The grandmothers had prepared her. Little Flower had been devastated, but relied on her strength, saying, just as she had said many seasons ago, that he still lived. This time, she knew he lived with the Great Spirit. Badger had told her of the promise he had made to Soaring Eagle to look after her and keep her safe. There was no reason to tell her of his love for her, she already knew. The two of them spent much time together, talking of their lives with the Hillabee Chieftain. Both had loved him deeply.

Slowly Little Flower would smile again. Three seasons had passed since the death of Soaring Eagle and Little Flower continued to be the strength of the family. She and Morning Star and Little Deer were hoeing their garden when Little Deer noticed that her mother seemed to have problems breathing and looked pale. "My mother?" she asked. Do you feel sick? Is something wrong?"

Little Flower looked somewhat dazed, but smiled and answered, "I am fine. I think I may have gotten too warm. I will go sit in the shade for a while." After the evening meal, which the family still shared together, Little Flower had another spell similar to the earlier one. Once again, she had said she was fine and not to worry.

The next morning Little Flower told her family that she had dreamed of Soaring Eagle. That he had stood high on a hill, his arms open wide and called her name. Morning Star had once again looked into her crystal and prepared her family for what she knew would come. After the evening meal, Little Flower said she needed to go to the river, that she wanted to see the sun set and to herself, she added, one final time. Turning back to her family, she removed a strand of white beads from her neck and gave them to Little Deer. And then with a strand of blue beads, turned to Morning Star saying, "These belonged to your grandmother Sunflower Woman. She told me long ago to give them to you." She kissed both daughters and walked toward the river and the setting sun. Little Flower was buried beside Soaring Eagle and they again sang Amazing Grace.

The death of Little Flower had left a terrible void in the lives of Little Deer and Morning Star. They had depended on her strength, her courage and guidance. She was always there for them and now she was gone. Morning Star, needing the solace of the grandmothers, went to the favorite place by the river where her parents had spent much time over the years and the place where they both had walked the path. She sensed the presence of her mother.

Morning Star leaned against a tree beside the river and watched the slow-moving water flow by. The warm sun lulled her, and she felt herself slip into the place she needed to be to commune with the grandmothers. They were slow about appearing and Morning Star drifted into a deep sleep. Abruptly, she heard the sharp report of gunfire and blood-curdling yells and smoke all around. Soldiers dressed in blue and gray were charging at each other. She saw her own people, some with feathers in their long hair leading the way.
The smoke cleared and she saw her mother, Little Flower and grandmother Sunflower Woman. "Morning Star be strong. Prepare our people for what is to come. They will again be divided and fight against each other as they have done in the past," then they were gone. Morning Star rubbed her eyes, not understanding the vision she had seen.

Morning Star slowly walked back to her cabin, wondering what the grandmothers were telling her. Seeing the strange look on her face, Hawk asked, "Star, did you see the grandmothers?"

"Yes, but I do not understand the meaning of my vision. Hawk, have you heard of men wearing blue and gray going into battle?"

"I have, "her husband answered, "Men from the north and men from the south are in a big argument. Some are talking about the south pulling out of the United States."

"Why, would they do that?" Morning Star asked, puzzled.

"I am not sure, that I understand," Hawk continued.

"This will affect us," Morning Star sadly said.

Chapter Thirty-Seven
1861
There's Gonna Be Some Fightin'

The ten and eleven-old daughters of Morning Star and Hawk were happily playing in their yard with the grandsons of Mr. Walker when a group of young men rushed up the road in the direction of Tallassee Town. "Hey," one of the young boys yelled out. "Where are y'all going in such a hurry?"

We's going up to Tallassee to muster up. There's gonna be some fightin' and we wanna be part of it," one of the young men yelled back without stopping.

"Mama, Mama," the youngest daughter called out to Morning Stat as she came out the door of her cabin to see what the clamor was all about. "Those men said somebodies fightin' and they are going to fight too. Papa won't go fight, will he?"

Morning star patted the dark head of her daughter and smiled, thinking how the children now spoke like the white children they played with. "No, your father will not go fight," she answered, "I hope."

Hawk, Horse Stealer and Coyote had gone into town to pick up supplies for Mr. Walker. The merchants were all accustomed to seeing the Creek men and enjoyed talking with them. Hawk noticed that there seemed to be more activity in town today and asked what the commotion was all about.

"Well, ya know I told y'all a while back that the states here in the south have separated themselves from them up north. Now, there's gonna be some fightin' and men are joining up with the southern army. The old man behind the counter laughed and continued, "Don't speck it will take long for our boys to straighte 'em out."

Returning back home, Hawk had told Morning Star what was going on and what the merchants had told them. Morning Star then pulled her crystal from her pocket. Streaks of red immediately filled the stone. "I fear my Hawk," Morning Star

Dance With the Spirits

began slowly, "This battle will become many and will last for several seasons. People here in the southland will suffer much and a great number of people on both sides of the battles will die." She paused, "The entire country, including our people will know sadness, division and hardship because of these battles."

The prediction of the crystal would continue to be accurate. Just as the Creek people had been divided many seasons past when some had chosen the white man's way of life and others chose the traditional life of their people, division would occur again. Most of the old ones who had fought in the battles of the Creek Wars of 1813 were gone and the younger ones had no memories of the sadness and hardships that changed a way of life for the Creek people. Some still remembered and were reluctant and afraid. They wondered if their fate would be the same and some wondered why the Creek people should be involved in the war of the white man.

Opothle Yahola was considered an old chief now and many of his people were surprised when he sided with the northern states instead of the south. He was, after all, one of the, if not the wealthiest of all chiefs in Indian Territory. His wealth had been made with the help of his many black men. He had told those who had questioned his continued support of the federal government that it had been the people of Georgia and Alabama who took the land of the Creek. It had been those people who had forced them to leave and who now owned the land. He would not fight with them and besides the government from the north had promised to help the Creek people.

Others had a different opinion, supporting the plantation owners who had promised them an Indian state of their own if the Confederacy, the name they now called themselves, won the war. A division was created and as before divided families with members taking different sides.

Many black, both free and those still owned by the Creek and other tribes in Indian Territory gathered along with Creek Union supporters at the plantation home of Opothle Yahola for protection. He and other chiefs requested help from the white fathers in Washington for the Indians who had gathered there. They were told that the United States could not and would not assist them in Indian Territory and they should move on to Fort Row in Kansas for protection and support.

In November of 1861, former United States Indian agent, Confederate Colonel Douglas Cooper led 1,400 men to Indian Territory. Many of these men were pro-Confederate Indians and some were acquaintances of Chief Opothle Yahola. Their purpose was to ask the chief to support the Confederacy. If he refused, he and his followers would be driven from Indian Territory. Opothle Yahola unfortunately refused and continued to trust the promise made by the United States government. He led his people to Kansas with the Confederate troops hot on his trail. This pursuit resulted in three battles.

In their haste to leave, many of their supplies were left behind. Opothle Yahola's group which numbered nine thousand did manage to drive back the Confederates in one of the battles. The southern troops soundly defeated the Union supporters in the final battle in December. Opothle Yahola lost two thousand of this people, either in battle, sickness or from the terrible cold on their journey to Kansas. Again, most of the Creek people did not have warm clothing and shoes. Many were sick and hungry. When they arrived at the fort, there were no provisions for the chief and his people. They were told to move on to another fort where they fared no better. Opothle Yahola and the Creek people had once again been deceived by the United States government and again they suffered and died just as they had in the Creek Wars of the past and on the trail where they cried.

Chapter Thirty-Eight
December 2018
Hard Times in the Southland

Minnie Raintree stood and stretched her arms, "Boys I'm hungry. How 'bout some lunch. I have ham and cheese left from breakfast and that will make good sandwiches."

"Sounds good to me Aunt Minnie Raintree," Matthew answered. "Do we need to bring in more firewood for you?"

"No, might need some later. But y'all can come help me make the sandwiches."

"You know we need to be on the road by four. We have early classes tomorrow," Matthew replied.

"I had rather stay here," Jacob chimed in, "It's lots more fun than class."

"It is that buddy, but you know we can't miss this class," Matthew laughed as he put ice in glasses decorated with orange and yellow Indian designs.

"Getting pretty close to the end of my story. I think we will be finished by then. Sure, wish y'all could stay. This has been so much fun," Minnie Raintree added as she sat down. "Think I will begin while we eat, if that's alright with y'all?"

Both boys nodded, "Aunt Minnie Raintree, what happened to Chief Opothle Yahola?" Matthew asked, taking a bite of his sandwich.

"Sad, it was so sad," Minnie Raintree answered. "Opothle Yahola was heavy hearted about his decision to side with the Yankees and the way it turned out for his people. His daughter was not strong enough and she along with many others died that winter."

"Was she the wife of Soaring Eagle and Little Flowers son, Fox Slayer?" Matthew asked.

"Yes, yes she was," Minnie Raintree answered, wiping a tear from her eye. "Fox Slayer joined up with the Union Army. Little Deer and Morning Star never heard from him again.

Dance With the Spirits

The twins of Morning Star sided with the Confederates. One of them took a Minni ball to his leg and always walked with a limp after that. Coyote also fought alongside the twins. He came home safely, but never talked much about what he had seen."

"So, the family was split and were on different sides?" Jacob asked, his eyes wide with interest.

"They were, and as if they had not been through enough already, seems like most of the family that remained in Indian Territory sided with the Union and they suffered most. The daughters of Soaring Eagle and Little Flower and their families fared much better," Minnie Raintree continued.

"Did they all stay on the Walker farm?" Matthew asked, "And, did any battles take place near here?"

"Yes, the family remained on the Walker place. As it was in all the Southland, times were bad, very bad, but they did have food. And yes, there were a couple, I think they were called skirmishes," Minnie Raintree said, pouring more tea into their glasses. "Y'all know the old mill up in Tallassee supplied cloth for the soldier's uniforms and also their tents."

Both boys shook their heads, "Never heard that," Jacob answered.

"What did they teach y'all in school?" Minnie Raintree asked, laughing. "Well, did you know that near the end of the war, the mill was made into an armory and they made carbines for the Southern Army? Some of the best rifles ever made, they were. Well, the Yankee Army wanted to destroy the rifles and there was about 500 of them, and that's what brought them to the Tallassee area. Surely, you know that the railroad tracks were destroyed, and all of the pretty houses were burned on up the road near to where y'all go to school?"

Again, both boys shook their heads. "Aunt Minnie Raintree, I guess we were not paying good attention when we studied the Civil War," Matthew answered sheepishly.

"Matthew," Minnie Raintree said sharply, "It was called the War Between the States. It was not a civil war," she smiled.

"Now, I will quickly finish this part of our story and get back to our family. You asked about battles here. There were two. One called the Battle of Chehaw, where cadets from the University of Alabama along with some local militia from Tuskegee fought the Yankees the best they could. Then there was the Battle of Franklin. The Yankees were trying to find the Tallassee Armory," Minnie Raintree laughed, "They were on the wrong side of the river, so they couldn't find it. Anyway, the carbines had already been packed up with plans to ship them to Macon, Georgia. To this day, no one knows what happened to them. Some folks say the Yankees confiscated them and others say they were buried under the old mill. Three or four are in museums now, but that's enough about that. I've got to move on so y'all can go," Minnie Raintree paused, "Matthew, would you please go out and bring in some more firewood?" she asked.

"I'm getting a little chilly. Want take much longer before I'm finished, but I do not want to leave anything out," she smiled, "It is all so important."

Chapter Thirty-Nine
Dance of Minnie Raintree

When the boys returned with the wood, Minnie Raintree had mugs of hot chocolate ready. "I know it's getting late in the day, so let's get started," Minnie Raintree said, sitting down in her chair. "Here we go. News traveled slow back then, and it was after the terrible war was over before the family found out that old Chief Opothle Yahola had walked the path in March of 1863. He was buried beside his daughter at a fort of the white man in Kansas. He never came back home," she paused, "What a life he lived. Our people, both in Indian Territory and those that were here, slowly, like the white people, pulled their lives back together. The little girls of Morning Star grew up and both married their playmates, the Walker brothers. They continued to live on Walker land. They were happy and prosperous. On the other hand, our people in Indian Territory again faced difficult times when the white people decided they wanted that land too. The Indian people lost much of their land and were forced to live on reservations."

Minnie Raintree laughed, "You know some folks always want what does not belong to them. They still do today, don't they? That brings us to modern times, of course, I have already told you about how me and," smiling at Matthew, "And you are connected with all the wonderful people I have told you about?"

"One more thing about our people, Aunt Minnie Raintree," Matthew asked. "What happened to Morning Star and her sister?"

"Oh, yes," Minnie Raintree answered, "Morning Star and Hawk both lived well into their eighties and Little Deer and Horse Stealer lived long lives as well. Of course, being older than Morning Star, both walked the path to the Great Spirit sooner. All were buried on Walker property."

"Do you know where?" Jacob asked.

"No, the Walkers owned much land." Minnie Raintree answered, "Maybe you and Matthew can locate their graves one day."

"Aunt Minnie Raintree," Matthew asked, "Did any of our Creek people ever come back here to live or just to visit?"

"Oh yes, many came back," Minnie Raintree smiled, "Just like our family. They settled near other Creek families and some married white men and white women. Some hid out deep in the woods. You know the government would send our people back to Indian Territory well into the twentieth century. We were shamed and made fun of, just because we were Indian."

"You are kidding!" Jacob exclaimed.

"No, my boy, I am not. I am happy to see that nowadays people want to be of Native American descent."

"Sure, want to find me some Indian ancestors," Jacob replied.

"Maybe harder than you think, Jacob," Minnie Raintree answered. "Oh, let me tell you about this. Creek people have always come back for short periods. Seems like they were looking for something. One event in particular comes to mind, one of which I was fortunate enough to see. The Tallassee folks up in town were having some sort of special day and many Creek people from Oklahoma were invited to come. A group of us went down to the boat landing just below Tallassee. That's the place where the natural bridge is. Our people had used those rocks to cross the river for hundreds of years. Oh boys, I wish y'all could have been there. One of the Creek men, dressed just as one of his ancestors, walked out on the rocks. He took a feather, either from an eagle or hawk from his hair. He pointed the feather in all four directions, said something in our native tongue and released it into the flowing river. I felt like I had gone back into time and watched Soaring Eagle perform a sacred ritual." Minnie Raintree paused, again wiping a tear from her cheek. Suddenly the vibrant woman had a faraway look in her eyes as if she was suddenly in a different place and time.

Smiling, Minnie Raintree touched the blue beads that hung

from her neck. "Well boys, that's my story. I hope you enjoyed hearing about my," looking at Matthew she smiled, "Our people as much as I enjoyed telling you about them. Each one, Sunflower Woman, Soaring Eagle and Little Flower and their children, especially Morning Star and the others, and, oh yes, don't forget about Badger."

"Aunt Minnie Raintree," Matthew interrupted, "What happened to Badger? You did not tell us about him."

"Oh, Badger," Minnie Raintree said with a sigh, "He was a good man. He loved Little Flower from afar for most of his adult life. He also loved and respected Soaring Eagle. He never touched her," she smiled, "Except that one time many, many years past when he thought Soaring Eagle did not live. He would never do anything dishonorable. He lived a year or two longer than Little Flower. He continued, as he always had, looking after the family. When he walked the path to the Great Spirit, he was buried on the big hill overlooking the river right beside Soaring Eagle. The children thought he would have wanted it that way. They were all special people that lived in a different, magical time. I often feel that I am a part of that time and that I will soon join them."

"Aunt Minnie Raintree," Matthew admonished. "Don't say things like that!"

"My boy," Minnie Raintree began, "I have lived for over one-hundred and two seasons. My time here cannot be much longer," she smiled and looked at the clock, quietly ticking on the wall. "Three-forty-five, well, I see that I did finish the story just in time for you boys to get your things together and be heading up the road." Laughing she continued, "Sure you boys don't want to finish your education up at Alabama?"

"No Mam," Matthew answered, "I think we are doing just fine at Auburn."

"I know, and I am proud of you both. It has been a wonderful weekend for me," Minnie Raintree said, becoming serious. "Thank you so much for coming and spending time with this old woman and listening so closely. The story needed to be told, Matthew," she said, slowly rising from her chair and going to a cedar chest, the patina showing that it was very old and had been used for many years. The old woman turned back to the boys, holding a leather-bound book with frayed edges and securely tied with a faded blue ribbon. "Matthew, I would like for you to have this. I have been saving this to give to the right person at the right time and you are that person." Tears freely ran down her face that now seemed old and tired. "Matthew, this is the written words of the story I have told you. Treasure this book and tell our story to others of our family and all who want to know. Tell them about the Creek people who lived so long ago. I have, just last night made the final entry." Standing on her tip toes, Minnie Raintree kissed Matthew on his cheek and gave him the book.

Matthew took the worn book from her hands and looked deeply into her faded eyes, that only a little while ago had sparkled with joy and humor. "Aunt Minnie Raintree," he spoke softly, "I love you."

"I love you, Matthew," turning to look at Jacob, "And you too, Jacob, thank you for wanting to know my story."

The boys packed up the few things they had scattered around the small cabin and prepared to leave. Neither wanted to go. "Aunt Minnie Raintree," Matthew said as he started his truck, "We will come back soon, very soon."

Minnie Raintree smiled as she waved at the boys and quietly said to herself, "I will no longer be here. I will Dance with the Spirits. I can hear their call and I hear the call of the owl."

****

The following afternoon Matthew received a text from his cousin. Minnie Raintree Walker Harper had passed away. She had been found in the old cotton field near her home clutching a strand of blue beads. Matthew openly cried when he received the message. He knew that Minnie Raintree did not just die.

She had heard the drums call and had walked the path of the Great Spirit. Matthew knew she had been reunited with her family, Soaring Eagle, Little Flower and Morning Star. She now would Dance with the Spirits.

The End

Epilogue

When I completed *Just a Cotton Field*, I did not know if the story would continue. One day, for no particular reason, a voice from inside of me seemed to say, "Finish my story." I think that voice might have been Little Flower. For my birthday, my husband Randall had given me a great book on the removal of the Creek people, which included the Tallassee and the Tuckabatchee. So, I had the information I needed and began to write. The story needed to be finished.

The path taken by Soaring Eagle and his family was the actual route of the Creek people as they left the Tallapoosa River Valley. They did indeed go through the towns of Wetumpka, Maplesville, Centerville, Tuscaloosa and Tuscumbia before crossing the corner of Mississippi into Tennessee, then Arkansas and finally to Indian Territory. The men who led them from Tallassee were real life people, including Dr. Bussy and of course Barrent Dubois.

The difficulty crossing the Mississippi River was true as well as the weather conditions. The Creek people were plagued by the white man's attempt to sell them whiskey and take their money away on trumped up charges, just as Soaring Eagle's group experienced. The personal items of the Creek people of Tallassee were not returned to them as they really did rot on a steamboat in the Gulf of Mexico. Women were forced to pick up corn from the ground intended for the soldier's horses for their own nourishment. There were many hardships and the Creek people suffered greatly with much sadness and death.

There were those who either did not go or came back just as Soaring Eagle and his family did. Trader Walker actually lived and became a wealthy landowner. He was related, and some sources say, married to the daughter of Tuckabatchee Chief Big Warrior. Even though there is little evidence to support kinship to Trader Walker, the Walker family still owns land today in the Tallapoosa River Valley.

The story of Soaring Eagle and Little Flower embodied the real-life plight of the Creek people. The visits from the grandmothers and the *Dance With the Spirits* were, of course, fictional, although the Creek people did deeply believe in the spirits. So maybe, just maybe, they did exist. Soaring Eagle and his family became real to me as I wrote their story, so real in fact, tears came to my eyes and I had chill bumps when Soaring Eagle, Little Flower and then Minnie Raintree walked the path to Dance With the Spirits.

Acknowledgments

Bending Their Way Forward
Creek Indian Removal and Documents
Edited and Annotated by
Christopher D. Haveman

The Five Civilized Tribes
Grant Foreman

The Old Beloved Path
William W. Winn

Maps and Photograph Location
Tallapoosa River Photo, Macon County, Alabama
Route of Creek Removal Map, Bending Their Way Forward
Trail of Tears Paintings, Fine Art America
Canadian River Map and Photo, Oklahoma Historical Society
20th Century House at Tuckabatchee, Hendrix Family Property
Home of Mrs. Ophelia Walker near Millstead, Alabama
Downtown Tallassee Water Tank Photo, Site of Old Cemetery on the Hill

Cover Photograph
Author's Personal Artifact Collection

Editing
Thanks to my special friend Jeanna Kervin for her editing assistance and to Fred Randall Hughey, my wonderful husband. Without his help, patience and love my dream to write about Native American people could never have been fulfilled.

The Tallapoosa River. Native American people lived along it's banks for thousands of years. Their Spirit remains here today. Photo taken from the Macon County, Alabama bank of the Tallapoosa near the original Trader Walker property. This could have been Soaring Eagle's favorite spot.

Dance With the Spirits

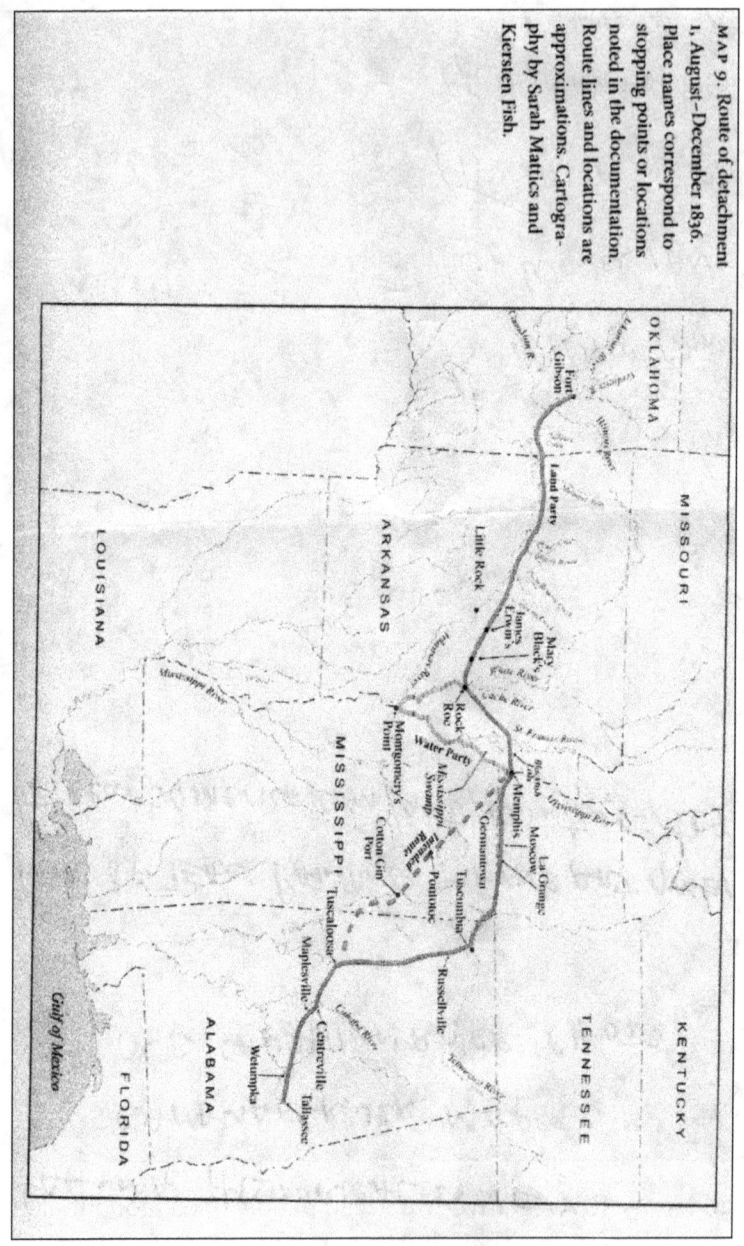

Map showing the actual route of removal taken by the Talisi and Tuckabatchee people when they were forced to leave their home in Alabama in September of 1836.

Realistic paintings of the Creek and Cherokee as they walked the trail where they cried.

Dance With the Spirits

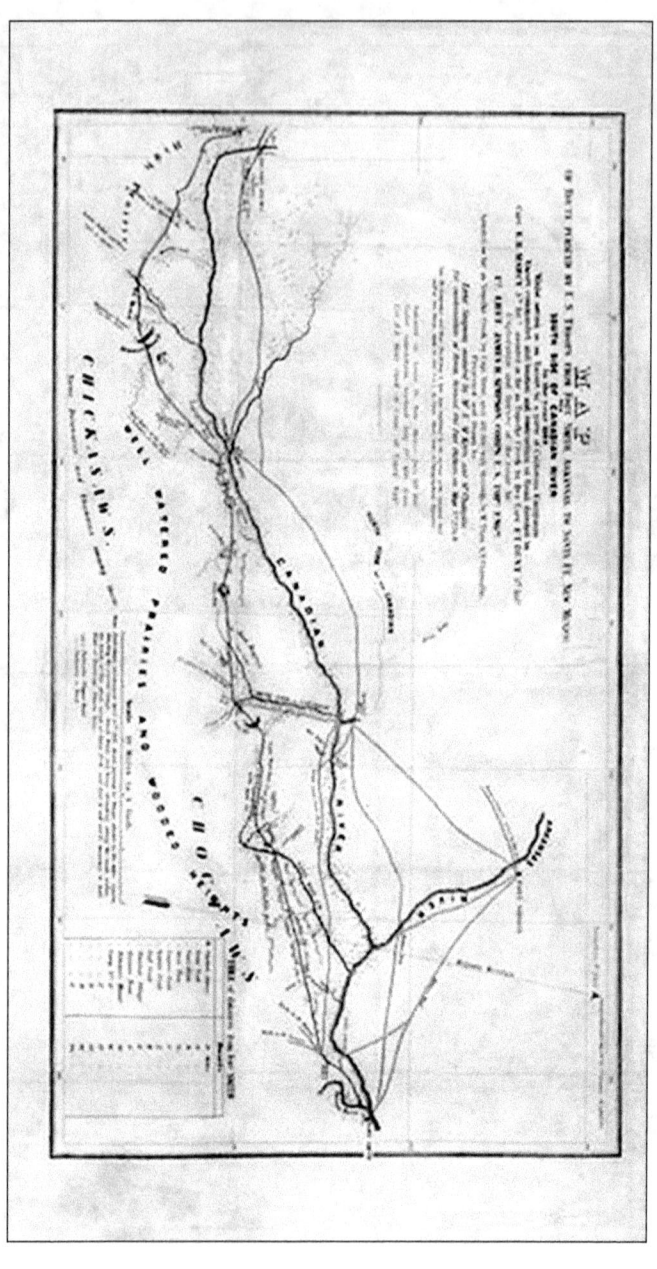

Canadian River, Oklahoma map showing where many Southern tribes settled.

1800s photo of Canadian River, Oklahoma where the Creeks were forced to live.

Photo of present-day abandoned house at Tuckabatchee which would have resembled the home of Minnie Raintree in the cotton field where she danced with the Spirits.

Minnie Raintree house at distance.

The home of Mrs. Ophelia Walker located near Millstead, Alabama. It was preceded by several homes on the site and was perhaps a stage coach stop in the past. There is no definitive proof the present-day Walker family is descended from William "Trader" Walker, however for several generations the Walkers have lived on land which could have previously been a part of Trader Walker's property.

Debra Hughey

Site of old Indian and early white settlers cemetery. In later days the City of Tallassee, Alabama, reinterred many of the white graves, including Barrent Dubois, to Rose Hill and other cemeteries. It is believed the Indian burials still remain beneath the water towers and the surface of Barnett Blvd.

— More Books By Debra Hughey —

People of the Townhouse $19.95

    Debra Hughey is considered by many as the expert of Creek Indian culture and history in the Tallapoosa River Valley of East-Central, Alabama. Discovering new things about the original inhabitants of Tallassee, Alabama, has been her life-long passion.

The Owl and The Horseshoe $14.95

    Debra Hughey chronicles the typical Creek village prior to the decisive Battle of Horseshoe Bend in 1814, providing the reader with an intimate capsule of Creek life in the Hillabee Village of central Alabama.

Spirit of the Red Stick Women $14.95

    Debra Hughey tells of the aftermath of General Andrew Jackson's 1814 victory over the Red Stick Warriors at the Battle of Horseshoe Bend which ended Creek Indian dominance in Alabama. Approximately, 1,000 Creek men were killed at the Horseshoe, leaving a few old men and the Creek women and children refugees in their own country. Debra Hughey's story of the plight of the widows and orphans of the massacred Red Stick Warriors is one which has likely never been told.

Just A Cotton Field $14.95

    Just A Cotton Field is the third in a series of the story of the Hillabee Chieftain Soaring Eagle and his family. The great influx of white settlers continued to change the lives of the Creek people and was even a threat to their existence. *Just A Cotton Field* is the story of the tremendous hardship and struggle in the years prior to the removal of the Creek people.

www.ingramcontent.com/pod-product-compliance
Lightning Source LLC
Chambersburg PA
CBHW052136110526
44591CB00012B/1740